CREATIVE BIBLE LESSONS
IN GENESIS

PERFECT FOR SUNDAY SCHOOL, YOUTH MEETINGS, SMALL GROUPS, AND MORE!

HOON KIM

ZONDERVAN®

Youth Specialties
.com

ZONDERVAN.com/
AUTHORTRACKER
follow your favorite authors

CREATIVE BIBLE LESSONS IN GENESIS

HOON KIM

Creative Bible Lessons in Genesis
Copyright © 2007 by Hoon Kim

Youth Specialties products, 300 S. Pierce St., El Cajon, California 92020, are published by Zondervan, 5300 Patterson, S.E., Grand Rapids, Michigan 49530.

Library of Congress Cataloging-in-Publication Data
Kim, Hoon, 1971-
  Creative Bible lessons in Genesis / Hoon Kim.
    p. cm.
  Includes bibliographical references.
  ISBN-10: 0-310-27093-6 (pbk.)
  ISBN-13: 978-0-310-27093-5 (pbk.)
  1. Bible. O.T. Genesis—Study and teaching. I. Title.
  BS1239.K56 2006
  222'.110071—dc22

                                                                              2006024013

Creative Team: Dave Urbanski, Kristi Robison, David Conn, Heather Haggerty and Janie Wilkerson
Cover design by Holly Sharp
Printed in the United States of America

07 08 09 10 • 15 14 13 12 11 10 9 8 7 6 5 4 3 2

DEDICATION

To my dad and mom for teaching me perseverance and to my wife, Shelly, God's second greatest gift to me.

Soli Deo Gloria.

TABLE OF CONTENTS

INTRODUCTION

UNCHANGING TRUTHS IN CHANGING TIMES

The book of Genesis is about first things. It talks about the beginnings of creation, humanity, sin, and peoples. But it also does much more. Genesis gives us an explanation of why we do the things we do, as well as offers us hope through shadows. Though it is the first book of the Bible, it points us to the final chapter as well—the one you and I will get to write together concerning our eternity with God. Though the world may change, new philosophies arrive, and fads appear and disappear, we find security in the unchanging God that his Word reveals. What Genesis says about us and about reality transcends time and worldviews.

This book explores such things and attempts to unearth heart motives and issues through the accounts of ancient ones. Because postmodern youth resonate best with stories rather than propositional truths, I've tried to write these lessons with the whole story of God's redemptive-historical plan in mind to convey that the Bible *is* story and that truth is found within its stories.

KEY THINGS TO KEEP IN MIND

Plenty of material is available to help pastors and teachers become more effective small group leaders; however, you won't find it in this introduction. Here's why: Other people have said it better! Some resources I recommend are *The Ministry of Nurture* by Duffy Robbins, *The Youth Builder* by Jim Burns and Mike Devries, and a whole slew of material by Doug Fields available at www.simplyyouthministry.com. Check their stuff out. Below are some key teaching pointers that specifically go with the material prepared in this book.

Heart and mind: These studies are intended to teach easy-to-learn biblical truths and intellectually engage our students to see society and culture from a Christian worldview. I designed these lessons to make your students think critically and understand God's plan throughout history.

Customization: Every Bible study curriculum is created with an audience in mind. Realistically, the audience I had in mind when writing this material (even though it consists of teenagers) isn't *your* specific audience. So please feel free to customize the study according to your group. Though the different sections are labeled as openers, discussions, and closings, feel free to use each in whichever sequence or for whatever purpose you see fit.

Christ-centered: You will notice that almost every chapter in this book includes a section that talks about Jesus. I think this is crucially important in light of Luke 24:44, which reads, "This is what I told you while I was still with you: Everything must be fulfilled that is written about me in the Law of Moses, the Prophets and the Psalms." To make this ancient faith real to us and to our students, we need to explain how Jesus fulfilled the promises of God in the Old Testament.

Sin: As much as we love youth and desire to encourage them, at different points in our relational ministry, we need to come to grips with the fact that sin happens to us as much as we sin ourselves. Make sure you address sin issues as they arise, whether you commit or suffer from them, and always use the opportunity to bring in the good news of the gospel.

Prepare in advance: Some of the material in these lessons isn't suited for just showing up on Sunday morning and using the book sight unseen. Because of widespread biblical illiteracy and the resulting faith struggles of our students when they enter college, these studies are a little more in depth. Therefore, make sure you pray, prepare, and plan each lesson in advance.

ABOUT THE SECTIONS OF THE STUDIES

All the studies have been divided as follows:

    Big Idea: a summary of the main point(s) of the lesson for you

Openers: fun, creative ways to get the discussion started and your community engaged

Transitions: examples of simple statements you can use to go from one section to another

Discussions: the meat and potatoes of the lesson

I've tried to include both "questions only" and creative approaches to the lessons. Also, some of the same activities can teach different topics, so I offer diverse ideas to increase your discussion options.

Closings: final activities meant to apply the lessons at home or within the small groups or to help your kids meditate and reflect on what they learned

Making the lessons personal is the most important thing about this section.

Interesting Tidbits: Where I've included some necessary theological or historical notes to help you (and your students, if you think they'll be interested) process the lesson

Zipped Files: Concise summaries of special peoples' lives

Some of the lessons cover many Bible chapters. The Zipped File pages give background information and quick bios of main characters so that your group doesn't need to spend a large portion of the meeting reading. Verses are also included in case you want to go back and highlight some references.

A FINAL WORD

I pray that God will bless you and your students, that you will all grow in the image of our Creator, and as a result of these studies you will engage the world to his glory. Know that I spent about as much time praying God would bless you through these lessons as I did preparing them.

BIG IDEA

What does it mean that God is Creator? What does creation itself reveal about God? This lesson will teach students the general narrative of the creation account of Genesis 1 and basic implications about what that means for us today.

Note: Although evolution versus creation is one of the most debated topics in modern times, this lesson presupposes that God created everything. For a good overview of the discussion, begin with *The Case for a Creator* by Lee Strobel (also available in a student edition).

OPENER (OPTION 1: IMPROV CREATORS)

This section is meant to get your students talking and developing intimacy as a community and to simultaneously get them thinking about the concept of creation.

As your students gather, place colored clay in front of them. Initially, do not discuss what the clay is for nor what they are to make with it; simply let them know it is

YOU'LL NEED

- Bibles
- pens/pencils
- colored clay
- copies of **Quiz of Astronomical Proportions** (page 18)
- Milky Way® chocolate bars
- "Galaxy video from www.highwayvideo.com
- contemplative background music
- projection equipment and multimedia person
- copies of **The Creation Narration** (page 20)
- copies of **Massive If-Then Statements** (page 21)

available for them to use as they wish. As students start molding the clay into shapes, have them share what their weeks were like. Additionally, you can ask the students to describe their emotions about the week through clay figures.

After about 10 minutes of sharing, ask the students to describe what their creations are by saying things like—

- *Let's go around and describe what we created.*
- *How does what you made reflect you or perhaps your emotions?*
- *How is your creation different than when God created the universe?*

OPENER (OPTION 2: QUIZ OF ASTRONOMICAL PROPORTIONS)

Pass out copies of **Quiz of Astronomical Proportions** (page 18) and give kids about five minutes to complete them. Pass out Milky Way® chocolate bars to the students with the highest scores.

The answers to the quiz are as follows:

(1. a, 2. a, 3. a, 4. a, 5. b, 6. d, 7. a, 8. a, 9. c, 10. b)

After awarding the prize, review the astronomical facts by saying something like,

Imagine this data for a moment. In one second light can travel seven times around the earth. In one year the distance light travels is about 9.46×10^{12} kilometers—one light-year. Our Milky Way galaxy is about 100,000 light years in diameter, and there are possibly about 100 million galaxies in the universe, with each galaxy containing about 100 billion stars. The distance to the observable edge of the universe is 15 billion light years. Psalm 8:3 says God created the whole universe by a simple work of his fingers.

Now ask something like,

How does this knowledge affect your relationship with God?

Then say,

This same creator God became a human baby, lived 33 years, and was sacrificed for our sins. This all-powerful God was willing to die out of love for you. He has ushered us all into his presence today to discover him. Why don't we start with a word of prayer?

Invite some students to pray for the Bible study in light of the opener.

OPENER (OPTION 3: VIDEO INTRODUCTION)

Show a video that illustrates the sovereignty of God over creation and nature. (Highway Video has an excellent clip, sound included, titled "Galaxy." It is available for download from www.highwayvideo.com.) Simultaneously, play some contemplative background music that highlights the work of creation. Some options are "God of Wonders" by Third Day or "Wonderful Maker" by Chris Tomlin/Matt Redman.

Transition into the Bible study by inviting students to an interactive call and response. For a sample script see **Video Introduction: Call and Response** (page 19). As you or another leader closes the prayer of invocation, have students sit down and break into small groups, depending on the size of your group and the type of meeting you're holding.

DISCUSSION (OPTION 1: THE CREATION NARRATION)

Distribute copies of **The Creation Narration** (page 20). Allow the youth enough time to complete all the answers. Once the students are finished, regroup and go over the handout.

Then ask the following questions and have students include verses that support their answers.

1. **By what action did God create all things?**
(*Speaking.*)

2. **How many times does the author of Genesis say that God's creation was good? What do you think God may have meant?**
(*Six times. The created things were perfect as God made them.*)

3. **When the Bible says that God rested on the seventh day, what do you think that means? Was God tired?**
(*No, he was not tired. He used the day to admire all that he made.*)

4. **When did God say it was not good? Why do you think he said that?**
(*As man was made in the image of a Trinitarian God, a God involved in eternal fellowship with himself (Father, Son, and Holy Spirit), we ourselves were made for community. God therefore created us to be relational, but no one of Adam's kind was available.*)

5. **If God is the Creator, what must be true about him?**
(*Possible answer: He must be eternal, without beginning or end. He must be powerful, since he created all things by the power of his words. He must be creative, since he made all the different objects of creation. He must be wise and knowledgeable, since he must have also invented the physical laws (of science, math, etc.) behind all these. He is the owner of all of creation and all things come from him.*)

DISCUSSION (OPTION 2: CREATION DRAMA)

If your group of students is particularly bold and artistic, divide them into two to four groups and have them act out the creation account. Let the students know that they will not be using speech, except for one designated narrator. Give them enough time and freedom to use props and creative special effects. Tell students to act out animals and vegetation as well as light and darkness. Assign the following segments as you see fit and limit their planning to about 15 minutes.

Act 1: Genesis 1:1-13   Act 3: Genesis 2:4-9

Act 2: Genesis 1:14-2:3   Act 4: Genesis 2:15-25

TRANSITION

Say something like,

> *This last exercise gave us a general overview of what happened on each day of creation and how God noted that everything, up until the discovery of Adam's loneliness, was good. On the seventh day God rested. Now let's go a little deeper and discover what it means that God is Creator. The fact that God is Creator and created everything in the universe has huge implications for our everyday lives that maybe we don't often think about.*

MASSIVE IF-THEN STATEMENTS

Ask students to turn to the New Testament, to the book of Colossians. Lead the group in reading Colossians 1:15-20 in unison. Now hand out copies of **Massive If-Then Statements** (page 21).

Say something like,

> *Let's go over some of the implications of this passage with some logical if-then statements. For example, IF God created and sustains everything, as Colossians 1:17 says, THEN he must also know everything. Catch that? He must know everything that goes on in creation, from where a dingo is hiding in Australia to what a barracuda is eating right now off the coast of Jamaica to whatever you have been going through this past week. In the space provided write down some things that God must know about what's going on in your life.*

Give kids about 20 minutes to think through the remainder of the if-then statements and reassure them that if they can't think of too many, you'll brainstorm more as a group. Once the allotted time is up, regroup and collect what each student has come up with on a writing board or large sheet of paper so all can see.

Possible answers are—

(If God made everything good, he is by nature good and has good things stored up for me. If God made everything out of nothing, he is powerful and able to do all the things that seem impossible to me. If God designed everything, he knows how things work, like physics, and why we should obey his laws. If God made everything, he owns everything, including our gifts, bank accounts, and time.)

Throughout this exercise encourage discussion and making the implications as personal as possible. Close this exercise by asking each student to write on the bottom of **Massive If-Then Statements** a summary of what this idea of God as Creator means to them.

TRANSITION

Prepare to close the lesson by saying something like,

We will study later on that although God created everything to be good, sin came into the world and caused the brokenness that we sometimes experience. But God wasn't defeated. God sent Jesus, his Son, to absorb the brokenness of creation and make those who believe in him new creations. In the same way that God made order out of what was formless and empty, Jesus brings healing and new life into what is broken by sin.

CLOSING (OPTION 1: SONG MEDITATION)

Ask students to close their eyes and meditate as they listen to "You Do All Things Well" by Chris Tomlin. If you choose, find and hand out the lyrics to the song.

CLOSING (OPTION 2: SONG MEDITATION WITH CLAY)

As the students listen to "You Do All Things Well" by Chris Tomlin, ask the students to reshape the clay they used at the beginning of the lesson as a response to the study.

CLOSING (OPTION 3: PARTNER PRAYERS)

Use this option if several kids shared some real-life struggles. As the students listen to "You Do All Things Well" by Chris Tomlin, encourage them to pray with each other in response to **Massive If-Then Statements**. Encourage your students to contact each other during the week to pray for the same topics over the phone.

QUIZ OF ASTRONOMICAL PROPORTIONS

1. The speed at which light travels is about

    a) 186,000 miles/second
    b) 18,600 miles/hour
    c) 186,000 kilometers/second
    d) 55 miles/hour

2. In one second light can travel

    a) seven times around the earth
    b) from the sun to earth
    c) from the moon to earth
    d) from New York City to Los Angeles

3. The 1995 blockbuster space movie starring Tom Hanks was called

    a) Apollo 13
    b) Apollo Ono
    c) Apollo 15
    d) Apollo Creed

4. One light-year is

    a) a distance of about 9.46 x 1012 kilometers
    b) how much a photon ages in a year
    c) equivalent to 9.8 human years
    d) a year with not much to do

5. The Milky Way galaxy

    a) is filled with chocolate malt–flavored nougat and milk chocolate
    b) is 100,000 light-years in diameter
    c) is shaped like a four-pronged ninja star
    d) contains one central black hole

6. Which of the following is not a star?

    a) a supernova
    b) Alpha Centauri
    c) the sun
    d) Ben Affleck

7. The average galaxy contains

    a) 100 billion stars
    b) 10 million earth-like planets
    c) 10 billion stars
    d) 1 trillion solar systems

8. The universe (possibly)

    a) contains 100 million galaxies
    b) is in the shape of a ring
    c) is collapsing
    d) travels east to west

9. To reduce travel time Obi-Wan Kenobi would use

    a) warp speed
    b) fantastic speed
    c) light speed
    d) the fast-forward button

10. The distance to the observable edge of the universe is

    a) unknown
    b) about 15 billion light-years
    c) unclear due to astro-fog
    d) about 150 billion miles away

VIDEO INTRODUCTION: CALL AND RESPONSE

Before your meeting have someone familiar with multimedia prepare the following script for projection. Edit as you see fit. Make sure each line is on a different page and that you use an overall dark background, so that the yellow and white are visibly different. Use a heavy font such as Impact and make sure you don't rush through the verses. Also, make sure there is some high-energy background music.

- IN THE PRESENCE OF OUR CREATOR GOD LET'S GATHER OUR VOICES AND PRAISE HIM.
- IF THE FOLLOWING TEXT IS IN WHITE, THE GUYS WILL READ IT ALL TOGETHER.
- IF THE FOLLOWING TEXT IS IN YELLOW, THE GIRLS WILL READ IT ALL TOGETHER.
- IF THE TEXT IS IN ANY OTHER COLOR, DON'T READ IT ALOUD.
- [other color] READY FOR A TEST?
- [white] KNOCK, KNOCK.
- [yellow] WHO'S THERE?
- [white] GOD.
- [yellow] GOD WHO?
- [white] THERE IS ONLY ONE GOD. WHO DO YOU THINK THIS IS?
- [other color] THAT WASN'T A JOKE.
- [other color] GOOD JOB. HERE WE GO AGAIN....
- [white] O LORD, OUR LORD, HOW MAJESTIC IS YOUR NAME IN ALL THE EARTH! YOU HAVE SET YOUR GLORY ABOVE THE HEAVENS.
- [yellow] FROM THE LIPS OF CHILDREN AND INFANTS YOU HAVE ORDAINED PRAISE BECAUSE OF YOUR ENEMIES, TO SILENCE THE FOE AND THE AVENGER.
- [white] WHEN I CONSIDER YOUR HEAVENS, THE WORK OF YOUR FINGERS, THE MOON AND THE STARS, WHICH YOU HAVE SET IN PLACE,
- [yellow] WHAT IS MAN THAT YOU ARE MINDFUL OF HIM, THE SON OF MAN THAT YOU CARE FOR HIM?
- [white] YOU MADE HIM A LITTLE LOWER THAN THE HEAVENLY BEINGS AND CROWNED HIM WITH GLORY AND HONOR.
- [yellow] YOU MADE HIM RULER OVER THE WORKS OF YOUR HANDS; YOU PUT EVERYTHING UNDER HIS FEET:
- [white] ALL FLOCKS AND HERDS, AND THE BEASTS OF THE FIELD,
- [yellow] THE BIRDS OF THE AIR, AND THE FISH OF THE SEA, ALL THAT SWIM THE PATHS OF THE SEAS.
- [white] O LORD, OUR LORD, HOW MAJESTIC IS YOUR NAME IN ALL THE EARTH!
- [yellow] O LORD, OUR LORD, HOW MAJESTIC IS YOUR NAME IN ALL THE EARTH!
- [other color] —PSALM 8
- [other color] LET'S BOW OUR HEARTS AND KNEES IN PRAYER. [OR IF YOU HAVE PEOPLE WHO CAN'T KNEEL] LET'S CLOSE OUR EYES IN PRAYER.

Have a leader say a prayer of invocation, calling to God for blessing over the meeting.

THE CREATION NARRATION

As you read the first two chapter of Genesis, fill in the following table.

DAY	WHAT WAS CREATED (INDICATE VERSE)	GOOD OR NOT GOOD? (INDICATE VERSE)
ONE		
TWO		
THREE		
FOUR		
FIVE		
SIX		
SEVEN		

MASSIVE IF-THEN STATEMENTS

After we read Colossians 1:15-20 together, you'll have 20 minutes to think through the remainder of the if-then statements. If you can't think of too many, don't worry; we will also brainstorm as a group.

Example:

IF God created and sustains everything (Colossians 1:17), he knows everything. Some sample answers are filled in for you.

IF GOD...	THEN HE...	SOME (IMPLICATIONS) ARE...	HOW THAT MAKES ME FEEL...
If God created and sustains everything (Colossians 1:17),	probably knows everything that's going on right now.	He knows where dingoes sleep in Australia, what a barracuda is eating off of the Jamaican coast, that my parents were fighting last night.	Reassured...I'm not alone.
If God made everything good,	must be powerful.		
If God designed everything,			
If God made everything,	owns everything.		
(Add your own.)			

CONCLUSION

After the group brainstorms, complete the following summary statement.

Since God is the Creator, I now know that he will...

_____

BIG IDEA

This lesson will teach students about the concept of the image of God and some implications of God's image. When students understand this, we can offer a timeless explanation of why we do what we do. Creativity, work, friendship, and love find their explanation in who God is. Therefore, since people are made in the image of God, only in God can we find ultimate satisfaction and significance.

OPENER (OPTION 1: STARS IN THE FAMILY)

There are plenty of parent-child celebrity pairs in sports and entertainment, and the Internet is full of photos of them. Collect photos of 10 such pairs from the Internet, print them out, and cut them up into individual photos (20 total). Somewhere on each photograph write a number (1-20).

Sit your students in a circle, hand out index cards, and pass the photos around (or have them on a bulletin board). Have kids match the celebrity pairs, writing down the numbers on their index cards. Award the student with the highest matches with a Milky Way chocolate bar by noting that he "got the most stars."

YOU'LL NEED

- Bibles
- pens/pencils
- 10 photos of parent-child celebrity pairs
- index cards
- Milky Way® chocolate bars
- pictures of students' parents when they were young
- copies of **Echoes in Hollywood** (page 29)
- copies of **Words Unpacked** (page 30-31)
- copies of **The Image Made Real** (page 32)
- copies of **Dig for Knowledge** (page 33)

continued next page

OPENER (OPTION 1: VARIATION)

Before the meeting tell your students to rummage through their parents' photo albums (with their parents' permission, of course) and bring in the oldest possible pictures of their parents. High school pictures or wedding pictures work great. Make sure you collect these pictures from the students before they have an opportunity to show them off to their friends. It may help to explain the activity beforehand so kids know why they shouldn't share.

Gather in a circle and lay the pictures out before the group, allowing the students to view all the pictures. Collect all the photos and proceed to show them one by one. Ask the group to guess whose parents these are. As each identity is revealed, ask the kids if they see any facial similarities between the parent(s) and the student. If both parents are in the picture, ask which one the student resembles more.

TRANSITION

Following this opener say something like,

> We all have parents whom we resemble in appearance and probably behavior. We may have their eyes, hair color, or even their ways of thinking. Though these characteristics are specific to our parents, Scripture says that we are all made in the image of one person, God. Understanding that we are made in his image gives us great insight and help for living. Today we're going to discover why we are relational and creative and what being an image bearer of God means.

OPENER (OPTION 2: ECHOES IN HOLLYWOOD)

Say something like,

> Because all humans are made in the image of God and sin has affected all of humanity, people from every corner of the earth somehow echo a need for God. Even though many do not want to admit to believing in God, movies and music echo this longing.

Hand out copies of **Echoes in Hollywood** (page 29) and if necessary explain some of the words under the Some Elements of the Gospel Story section.

Say something like,

> Everyone seems to be powerfully attracted to some of these elements. The following activity is meant to open up discussion on how even Hollywood blockbusters

express these gospel elements and how our longing for God is present everywhere. Take about 10 minutes to fill out the table.

Spend about 10 minutes sharing the findings from their tables. Invite the youth to question whether the underlying idea of the exercise is right. Invite your students to read from Acts 17:27-28 and then ask something like,

After reading these verses, what do you think is going on in the hearts of people everywhere?

TRANSITION

Say something like,

Most Hollywood blockbuster movies seem to have similarities that resonate with truths Christians have been familiar with for a long time. However, I'm not saying that the Bible is just another great story. God's story in the Bible is the ultimate, original, and unique story from which all other stories are born. Even people who don't believe in Jesus, because they are made in God's image, can subconsciously relate to the greatest story of all time—the story of a God who rescues people from sin's evil grasp.

OPENER (OPTION 3: MYSTERY CELL PHONE)

The purpose of this game is to highlight the idea that friendship, family, and work are supremely important in our lives.

Pass out index cards and have kids write down the first names (only) of the five people they call the most often, ranking them from 1 to 5 (1 being the person they call most, 5 being the person they call least). If some students don't make a lot of phone calls, simply ask them to write down the first names of the five people they connect with most during a typical week. After each student has written their names on the index cards, collect the index cards and shuffle them.

The object of the game is to guess which person each index card belongs to. Slowly read off names on each index card, starting with number 5 and descending to number 1. Allow students to shout out whom they think the card belongs to as you read.

At the end of the game say something like,

Our phones and who we call or connect with most reveal the fact that we are relational. We count on our friends and family for support and fellowship. Today we're going to discover WHY relationships mean so much to us.

TRANSITION

Say something like,

> *Isn't it interesting that all over the world, children at the beach will make sand-castles? Or that regardless of ethnicity or culture, people have an instinctive and powerful longing for friendship and love? The questions we want to answer, then, are: 'Why do we all want similar things? Why are we creative? Why does technology always push forward?' The answer is found in Genesis 1:26-30. In a nutshell, we were made in the image of a Trinitarian God who created and made order out of chaos. In many profound ways we resemble our heavenly Father! Think about it. God made the heavens and the earth, and he is perfectly three in one (Father, Son, and Holy Spirit), in communication and cooperation. The answer to the latter questions is that in many things we do, we mirror God.*

TRANSITION: WORDS UNPACKED
(FOR ALL OPENERS)

Hand out copies of **Words Unpacked** (pages 30-31) and say something like,

> *Perhaps you've heard that people are made in the image of God. Let's define some words using the handout Words Unpacked. These definitions will help us greatly as we go through the rest of our study.*

Go over each of the definitions and explain as much as needed.

DISCUSSION (OPTION 1: THE IMAGE MADE REAL)

Hand out copies of **The Image Made Real** (page 32). Instruct the students to write, in their own words, a definition for "image of God" and their guesses as to how sin affects this image. At your discretion allow kids to use the **Words Unpacked** help sheet. Have students read through and share their definitions of "image of God" and their three examples of how sin affects it.

Now say something like,

> *Listening to all your examples of sin, it seems as if things are pretty messed up in this world. Keeping this in mind, why do you think Jesus is called the Redeemer?*

After the students have given their answers, divide them into groups of three or four.

Instruct the small groups to complete the Group Questions section in 20 minutes or so, and when they're finished, have a student representative from each group share their answers.

Next ask the whole group these questions:

> • *If God would allow you to become exactly like Jesus in one way, what would you ask for?*

> • *In your opinion, what is the one thing about you that you feel is most similar to Jesus?*

> • *Where do you feel God is working in your life to make you more like Jesus?*

Image of God movie illustration—*The Lord of the Rings: The Fellowship of the Ring.* Show the clip from *Fellowship of the Ring* where the heroes are canoeing down the river (in the Special Extended Edition, disc two, scene 41 "The Great River," marker 1:10:47). At one point they paddle past massive stone statues representing the kings of Gondor. Show the clip until the heroes ground their canoes (marker 1:12:30, about two minutes).

Ask questions like—

> • *Who are these statues of?*

> • *Why do you think the statues were made so big?*

> • *Do you suppose these statues communicate something? What purpose do you think these statues serve in the world of the movie?*

Say something like,

> *In ancient times, Near East kings would put up statues of themselves to let people know who the ruling king was in a particular area. Amazingly, however, the Bible says in Genesis 1 and 2 that we are made in God's image and placed all over the world to let all creation know that the Lord is King of Kings.*

DISCUSSION (OPTION 2: DIG FOR KNOWLEDGE)

Hand out copies of **Dig for Knowledge** (page 33) and have your students answer questions in the spaces provided, using the Scriptures given. Read the Scriptures together and discuss the questions aloud, giving students time to write down their answers as you go. Then give kids about 10 minutes to capture the narrative in the master sketch. After that time have students share and describe their sketches.

TRANSITION

Say something like,

Today we've learned what the two basic meanings of the phrase 'image of God' are. Now let's apply this. We'll consider what other believers have concluded about the practical meanings of being made in God's image.

CLOSING: APPLICATIONS FROM FAMOUS FOLKS

Hand out copies of **Applications from Famous Folks** (page 34). Have the girls read the first quotation and the guys the second quotation. Discuss and unpack the meanings and implications of the two quotations, then challenge your group to live up to the ideals in the two quotations.

Hand out index cards to everybody and have students choose which of the four options they want to apply during the week. Make sure that you leave some time during the next lesson to follow up on their commitments.

Finally, have students sit in a circle, hold hands, and pray for their brothers/sisters on either side. Ask a volunteer to close the prayer time.

ECHOES IN HOLLYWOOD

All of creation is reaching for God in one way or another. Blockbuster movies become successes perhaps because they tap into the elements of the greatest story ever told—that of a Creator scorned by his creation who ultimately decides to make the greatest sacrifice to redeem his beloved people.

SOME ELEMENTS OF THE GOSPEL STORY

1. a redeemer/redemption (Isaiah 47:4)
2. someone who makes a huge sacrifice (Hebrews 9:28)
3. an outsider who comes in and fixes things up (John 1:9)
4. unconditional love (Jeremiah 31:3)
5. a restoration of peace (Revelation 21:5)
6. love conquering all (John 3:16)
7. good defeating evil (Revelation 20:7-10)

YOUR TURN

List your favorite three movies and see how many gospel elements are captured in the story line. Two examples have been given to get your brain juices pumping.

FAVORITE MOVIE	DESCRIPTION	GOSPEL ELEMENTS
The Matrix	People are looking for a Messiah figure who will awaken humanity and save it. Neo is the "chosen one" and has to make the ultimate sacrifice to save mankind.	1, 2, 3, 5, 7
Lilo and Stitch	An extraterrestrial menace attempts to destroy humanity. The unconditional love of a little girl changes the monster's heart, and they live happily ever after.	1, 3, 4, 6

WORDS UNPACKED

Were you ever unsure of the meaning of a word or only thought you kinda understood it? Sometimes even simpler words are sources of great confusion. We're going to take a few moments now to review and brush up on the following "Christian-ese" words.

GOSPEL—This word literally means "good news." The more specific meaning of the word refers to the message about the restoration of the kingdom of God and the believer through the life, death, and resurrection of the Lord Jesus Christ. All of humanity will be judged according to whether they receive or reject this good news.[1]

TRINITY—A theological term used to define God as an undivided unit expressed in God the Father, God the Son, and God the Holy Spirit. The Trinity is considered a divine mystery beyond human comprehension. Ultimately, God is one. And God has three distinct ways of being a redeemer but remains an undivided unit. God the Father designs creation and redemption, Jesus is sent to complete it through his death and resurrection, and the Holy Spirit works out salvation in the hearts of believers.[2]

REDEMPTION/REDEEM—These words convey the idea of paying a price to free or liberate someone from evil, oppression, and slavery. Another possible meaning is "to restore the initial worth of something, which was somehow lost." In the Bible redemption means restoration to an original condition, which is what happens to us through Jesus' sacrifice. Jesus paid for our sins to restore us into relationship with God. In another sense, since sin has corrupted creation itself, Jesus' work is a promise that one day all of creation, along with all believers, will be fully restored from decay and corruption (Romans 8:20-23).

GRACE—usually refers to a completely undeserved favor. When God bestows grace, it refers to the undeserved favor of God in saving us through the gift of his Son Jesus, who died in place of sinners.[3]

COVENANT—An promise in which one party solemnly pledges to bless or serve another party in some specific way. Sometimes keeping the promise depends upon certain conditions of the promise-giver. On other occasions the promise is unconditional (as in the case of Abraham in Genesis 12). The covenant concept is a central, unifying theme of Scripture, establishing and defining God's relationship to people in all ages.[4]

THE IMAGE OF GOD—The idea of the image of God is usually divided into two categories:

1. Humans share with God such qualities as personality, knowledge, morals, holiness, will, and sensibility. To be like God is to be patterned after him but at the same time to be qualitatively inferior to him.

2. Humankind is, in fact, the image of God. Humanity exercises divine control and influence in creation.

Therefore, humankind resembles God, even in a limited way, and stands in God's place to help rule his creation.[5]

1 Donny Mathis, *Holman Illustrated Bible Dictionary.*
2 Mathis, *Holman Illustrated Bible Dictionary.*
3 Jimmy A. Mililkin, *Holman Illustrated Bible Dictionary.*
4 Steven B. Cowan, *Holman Illustrated Bible Dictionary.*
5 E. H. Merrill, *The Image of God Dictionary of the Old Testament: Pentateuch*

THE IMAGE MADE REAL

In the space below write in your own words a definition of what being made in the image of God means.

In Genesis 3 we'll discover that sin has injured the image of God in people. What do you see in this world that seems to prove this damage? Give three examples.

1.

2.

3.

GROUP QUESTIONS

With your Bibles look up these verses and answer the questions that follow each set of verses.

2 CORINTHIANS 4:4   **COLOSSIANS 1:15**   **HEBREWS 1:3**

According to the above passages who is Jesus?

COLOSSIANS 3:9-10   **EPHESIANS 4:22-24**

According to the above passages what are believers to do?

2 CORINTHIANS 3:18   **ROMANS 8:28-29**

According to the above passages what is God doing in us?

DIG FOR KNOWLEDGE

As a group we will read Genesis 1:26-31 and take time to answer the questions in the spaces provided.

GENESIS 1:26-27

1. When God says "let US" and "OUR image," who do you think he's referring to?

2. What do you think God means when he commands people to "rule over" the earth?

3. Can you think of any animal or living thing that God missed?

4. When God created humans in "his image," he created them both male and female. What are some of the physical, personality, and role differences between males and females?
   —physical:
   —personality:
   —roles:

GENESIS 1:28

Make a list of God's commands to humankind from this verse.

GENESIS 1:29-30

What else does God give to people to rule over and subdue?

GENESIS 1:31

What is God's verdict about creation and his purpose for humankind? What do you think that means for us?

MASTER SKETCH

In the box provided below make a sketch of Genesis 1:26-31.

APPLICATIONS FROM FAMOUS FOLKS

"There are no ordinary people. You have never talked to a mere mortal...it is immortals whom we joke with, work with, marry, snub, and exploit—immortal horrors or everlasting splendors...Next to the Blessed Sacrament itself, your neighbor is the holiest object presented to your senses. If he is your Christian neighbor, he is holy in almost the same way, for in him also Christ...the glorifier and the glorified, Glory himself, is truly hidden." C. S. Lewis, *The Weight of Glory*[6]

"Marriage should not be avoided by Christians, but sanctified. Emotions should not be repressed, but purified. Sexuality is not simply to be shunned, but redeemed. Politics should not be declared off-limits, but reformed. Art ought not to be pronounced worldly, but claimed for Christ. Business must no longer be relegated to the secular world, but must be made to conform again to God-honoring standards. Every sector of human life yields such examples." Albert M. Wolters, *Creation Regained*[7]

APPLY

Pick one of the following four applications and write down your commitment on an index card. Make sure you place the index card somewhere visible and share your results at our next group meeting.

1. I will change the way I think of myself by _____.
2. I will change the way I think about and treat _____ by _____.
3. I will change the way I work and do homework by _____.
4. This week I will to talk to _____ about Jesus.

6 C. S. Lewis, *The Weight of Glory* (San Francisco: HarperCollins, 1976).
7 Albert M. Wolters, *Creation Regained: Biblical Basics for a Reformational Worldview* (Grand Rapids, MI: William B. Eerdmans Publishing, 1985).

CREATED FOR RELATIONSHIP

BIG IDEA

Think your youth are too young to talk about marriage? Think again! This lesson will teach your kids how to prepare for marriage and about some biblical dynamics they can begin absorbing into their lives right now to make the most of marriage when the day comes.

OPENER (OPTION 1: "A PAGE IS TURNED")

Find a copy of Bebo Norman's "A Page Is Turned" and hand out the lyrics. Before playing the song, say something like,

Today we are going to look at love and marriage, so let's listen to a song often played at weddings. As you listen to the song, try to picture what the boy, girl, and God are each individually doing.

Play the song. When the song finishes, ask the students—

YOU'LL NEED

- Bibles
- pens/pencils
- recording of the song "A Page Is Turned" by Bebo Norman
- index cards
- clear tape
- prize
- copies of **The First Love Story** (page 41)
- posterboard or easel
- copies of **A Romantic God** (page 43)
- cupcakes
- candles
- matches

• *Do you think either the boy or girl knew where their future spouse was as they were growing up?*

• *What was God's role in their relationship?*

• *What do you think the message of this song is?*

OPENER (OPTION 2: WHO'S HELPING WHO?)

Before your students arrive, prepare small index cards. For each pair on the **Who's Helping Who?** (page 40) sheet write each name on a different card and shuffle the cards. Create more pairs if your group size is more than 40. Using clear tape stick one card on each kid's back so the names are visible to others but not to the person with the card taped to her.

Students have to find their "helper" by first figuring out who they are. Kids may ask one question per person and then must move on to someone else. Kids may only ask yes or no questions. For example, "Am I an actor?" is acceptable, but "What professional field am I in?" is not because the answer is not yes or no.

Once a student correctly figures out who he is by asking something like, "Am I Batman?" have him find his famous partner.

Award the first pair to identify themselves with a prize of your choice. Depending on how many students you have and how many additional duos you can come up with, play more rounds of the game.

TRANSITION

Say something like,

> *Today we're going to look at the first famous human duo on earth. We're going to study how God created men and women differently and talk about the issues of romance and men's and women's differing roles in creation. To do that, let's open and read Genesis 2:4-7 and 15-25 together. Let's have the girls begin with verse four and alternate reading verses with the guys.*

Read Genesis 2:4-7 and 15-25.

DISCUSSION (OPTION 1: THE FIRST LOVE STORY)

Hand out copies of **The First Love Story** (page 41) and divide your group into teams of three or four. Assign a different section to each team and allow them to pick a summarizer who will share their answers when the groups join back up. Make sure each team also answers the All Together section.

After the teams finish their sections, regroup, review the answers, and then have the kids come up with a summary statement concerning what they think the purpose of relationships should be. Be prepared to write their ideas on a poster board or easel for all to see and then formulate a summary statement as a group.

DISCUSSION (OPTION 2: A ROMANTIC GOD)

Hand out copies of **A Romantic God** (page 43). As kids move through each section, have them share their answers and brainstorm what each secret principle might be. Then share the principle (listed in parentheses after each item) with the group.

Principle 1: First ask students to fill out the table. Then ask the following questions:

• *What do you think this says about God's interest in our love lives?*

• *How can you can apply this to your life?*

Brainstorm together what the first principle might be. Then have your students fill in principle 1. *(Know God is active in your relationships.)*

Principle 2: Say something like,

> While Adam was still single, God put him in charge of maintaining the garden. He was also put in charge of the tree of the knowledge of good and evil (Genesis 2:17). This might mean that singleness is a special calling.

Continue with the following:

• *Read 1 Corinthians 7:32-35. What do these verses teach?*

• *What do you think you can do now to prepare for marriage?*

• *How do you think serving prepares you emotionally, financially, and spiritually for marriage?*

Brainstorm together what the principle might be. Then ask your students to fill in principle 2. *(God prepares you through ministry and obedience.)*

Principle 3: Say something like,

> A famous author once wrote that becoming intimate without being married is like taking a bite of some delicious food, chewing and savoring it, and at the last moment spitting it out.

Continue with—

- *Check out verse 24. What do you think 'to be united' means? Is it just a physical union? How does this apply to the author's thought about food?*

- *What are some ways married couples become one?*

- *How does modern-day dating attempt to mimic marriage? Do you think it's dangerous? Why or why not?*

Brainstorm together what the principle might be. Then have your students fill in principle 3. *(God's plan for ultimate romance is found in marriage.)*

Then ask students to read Ephesians 5:22-33. Say something like—

- *How do these verses support principle 3?*

- *From the Ephesians verses, what are some ways men and women should show love to each other?*

- *How are marriage and ministry similar or different?*

Finally, brainstorm together what the summary principle might be. Then ask your students to fill in the summary principle. *(To maximize the joy of your future marriage, jump in and serve others now in some way because ultimately, marriage is ministry.)*

TRANSITION

Say something like,

> *God has a specific plan for romance and marriage. Genesis offers us a glimpse into the original picture of love and marriage. As we discussed last week, attraction to the opposite gender is a beautiful, God-ordained desire, rooted in who God is. Since God is a Trinitarian God and we are made in his image, we also long for relationship deep in our hearts. Genesis 2 provides us with some guidelines on how to maximize our joy.*

CLOSING (OPTION 1: QUALITIES IN A FUTURE HUSBAND/WIFE)

Have your group divide into same-gender pairs and instruct them to share with each other the five most important characteristics they'd want in a future spouse. (Make sure students focus on spiritual, character, and personality traits rather than on financial power or physical appearance.) As the students end their sharing time, close in prayer by asking each student to pray for—

• God to prepare whomever he has chosen as their future spouses according to their desired characteristics for a mate.

• God to prepare their own hearts to be godly for their future spouses.

CLOSING (OPTION 2: CUPCAKE TIME)

Know that this closing option will be repeated a few times throughout the course of this book to develop a sense of continuity and familiarity within your group. As the students have their time of sharing, play some music in the background.

Say something like,

> As we end today, let's have some time of reflection and sharing. Let's get together with members of the same gender and share and pray over this lesson together.

As much as possible have kids pair off with others who they don't know well.

Ahead of time prepare one cupcake per two students and place a candle in each cupcake. After the kids pair off, give each pair one candled cupcake, with the candle still unlit.

Find some mellow Christian music to play in the background and have teachers/volunteers go around and light the cupcakes. Turn down the lights.

Instruct students that as long as their candles are lit, they are to talk and share about themselves. Have one student share for half the candle and the other for the second half. Have students share struggles, things they are joyful about, and about their family and friends. Once the candles burn down, have the students pray for each other and split the cupcake.

CLOSING (OPTION 3: DEVOS ON LOVE)

Hand out copies of **Devos on Love** (page 44) as a guide to possible devotions for the week. Although there is no actual group activity connected with this option, encourage students to reflect on what Scripture teaches concerning biblical love on their own. Say,

> Here are some passages that you can meditate on during the next week. I've included several passages, but feel free to meditate on as few or as many as you want.

Follow up on their devotions the next time you gather. This option may also be used in addition to other ending options.

WHO'S HELPING WHO?

1. Batman and Robin

2. Adam and Eve

3. Ren and Stimpy

4. Itchy and Scratchy

5. Thelma and Louise

6. Mickey and Minnie

7. Dolce and Gabbana

8. Cain and Abel

9. Jacob and Esau

10. Jessica Simpson and Ashlee Simpson

11. John Stockton and Moses Malone

12. Michael Jordan and Scottie Pippen

13. salt and pepper

14. meat and potatoes

15. Frodo and Sam

16. Shane and Shane

17. cheese and crackers

18. Jackie Chan and Chris Tucker

19. (your pastor's name) and (spouse's name)

20. Matt Damon and Ben Affleck

Add more as your group requires.

THE FIRST LOVE STORY

Answer the questions in your small group's assigned section, as well as the All Together section, and pick someone to be the summarizer for your team. For the Conclusion section discuss your findings and brainstorm what you think is God's purpose for relationships.

SECTION 1: GENESIS 2:1-9

1. On what day does God form Adam? What does this tell you about humanity?

2. How does God form Adam?

3. Compared to the rest of creation, how is Adam's creation different? Do you think this is important? Why?

4. Sin doesn't slither in until Genesis 3. What might this tell you about work in 2:8-9 and 15?

5. What responsibility does God give Adam concerning the garden?

SECTION 2: GENESIS 2:15-18

1. What responsibility does God give Adam concerning trees?

2. Up to this point God declares everything he has created "good." In verse 18, we have the first "not good" thing. Why do you think Adam's being alone is declared "not good"?

3. What responsibility does God give Adam concerning animals?

4. What is the context for God's thinking that Adam's aloneness isn't good? In other words, which of Adam's activities reveal that being alone isn't good?

SECTION 3: GENESIS 2:20-23

1. On what day does God form Eve? What does this tell you about womanhood?

2. What responsibilities do you think Eve has at this point?

3. What do you think it means to be a "suitable helper"?

4. Beyond physical differences what do you think makes males and females different (if at all)?

5. "Suitable helper" doesn't mean the person is inferior. What is your opinion about the old question "Who wears the pants in the family?"

6. How does God create Eve?

7. Are there some things men can do that women can't? Are there some things women can do that men can't?

SECTION 4: GENESIS 2:23-25

1. What do you think are the top three characteristics Christians look for when searching for a life mate?

2. What do you think are the top three characteristics non-Christians look for when searching for a life mate?

3. What do you think it means to be "united" in verse 24? Is it just a physical union?

4. What do you think the purpose of sex is?

5. When people get united in marriage, in what ways do they become one?

6. Divorce rates today are quite high—what do you suppose is so hard about marriage?

7. When a couple leaves their fathers and mothers, what are some things they have to be able to do (or be) to live well without their parents?

ALL TOGETHER

1. What do you think these verses say about the ultimate purpose of relationships?

2. What do you think people in today's society see as the ultimate purpose of relationships?

CONCLUSION

According to Genesis, it seems that the ultimate purpose of relationships is:

A ROMANTIC GOD

First spend some time filling in the blanks on the following table. A passage is given on the right-hand side to help you navigate through Genesis 2. In each of the empty boxes write either *active* or *passive*.

	MAN'S ACTIVITY	GOD'S ACTIVITY	PASSAGE
Creation of Man			Genesis 2:7
Recognition of 'need'			Genesis 2:18
Creation of woman			Genesis 2:21-22
Adam's first encounter with Eve			Genesis 2:22

SOME PRINCIPLES TO MAXIMIZE YOUR FUTURE JOY.

They are left blank to see whether you can guess what they may be. Your leader will share the secret principles as you move through the lesson.

Principle 1: Know God _____.

Principle 2: God prepares you _____.

Principle 3: God's plan for ultimate _____.

READ EPHESIANS 5:22-33.

Summary principle: To maximize the joy of your future marriage, _____

_____

DEVOS ON LOVE

The passages below talk about love: God's love, friendship love, spousal love. As you read these verses throughout the week, know that you'll need all these kinds of love someday for your spouse. As you look at these Scriptures, try to answer three basic questions:

1. What does this passage teach about love?
2. What do I need to learn about love from these verses?
3. How has Jesus shown me this kind of love?

PASSAGES TO PICK FROM:

Ruth 1:16-18

Proverbs 4:23

Proverbs 31:10-31

Jeremiah 31:3-6

Zephaniah 3:14-17

Matthew 5:43-48

Luke 15:17-24

Romans 5:6-8

Romans 8:31-39

Romans 12:9-13

1 Corinthians 13

Hebrews 10:11-18

FAITH AND BROKENNESS

BIG IDEA

Students will walk away from this lesson with a better idea of God's involvement in their lives through biblical history, God's goodness and wisdom through blessings provided and withheld, and God's love and grace through the covering of his Son Jesus.

INTERESTING TIDBIT: TEMPTATION

Session four contains insight on the nature of temptation, sin, and how humans cope with sin. We are introduced to Satan and his desire to dishonor God and separate man from the Creator. When we fast-forward to the New Testament, we read that Jesus faced similar temptations during his 40 days of fasting in the desert. Although the strategies of the Enemy don't change throughout Scripture, we need to avoid becoming overconfident about Satan's lack of creativity. His tactics haven't changed because they're effective! The Enemy makes us doubt God and tempts us with pleasure, beauty, and power.

YOU'LL NEED

- Bibles
- pens/pencils
- lasagna
- ingredients for lasagna: mozzarella cheese, ricotta cheese, grated Parmesan cheese, olive oil, tomato sauce, oregano, thyme, basil, pepper, and salt
- copies of **Rusty Iron Chef** (page 51)
- copies of **His Story, My Story** (page 52)
- copies of **Howard Hughes** (page 53)
- copies of **Focus Shift** (page 54)
- copies of **Designer Fig Leaves** (page 55)

continued next page

You'll Need cont.

• red paint
• bowls
• tarp
• nails
• hammers
• wooden plank cross

OPENER: RUSTY IRON CHEF

Before the meeting prepare one pan of finished lasagna or purchase a ready-made lasagna. Also gather these ingredients in separate bowls: mozzarella cheese, ricotta cheese, grated Parmesan cheese, olive oil, tomato sauce, oregano, thyme, basil, pepper, and salt.

Pass out the **Rusty Iron Chef** handout (page 51) and have the youth try to guess the list of ingredients in a common meat lasagna and write these on the sheets. Tell the kids the winner will receive a piece of fresh lasagna. When the students finish, have them trade sheets with other students for scoring.

Read the list of ingredients and give five points for each correct ingredient. *(The 13 ingredients are: tomato sauce, ground beef, lasagna noodles, eggs, grated Parmesan cheese, ricotta cheese, mozzarella cheese, oregano, thyme, basil, salt, pepper, and olive oil to coat the pans.)*

Open the pan of fresh lasagna and sample the food. Say,

> *Congratulations to the winner(s) of tonight's Rusty Iron Chef contest! Come up and have some lasagna.*

Have the student or group (if you chose to split into smaller groups) with the highest score come up to receive lasagna and be the taste tester.

When the volunteer comes up, instead of the cooked lasagna, serve her the individual ingredients. Allow her to taste ricotta cheese, salt, olive oil, and fresh tomato sauce.

Read Romans 8:28 and say something like,

> *God tells us that in ALL things, he works for the good of those who love him.*

Emphasize how life is oftentimes unpleasant, but God works for good in all things. Show how some individual ingredients may not be particularly tasty while others are. Continue by explaining that God brings ALL things together and is able to make something delicious and amazing from individual, plain ingredients. Then say,

> *Today we will discover how to develop faith through the "tasties" and "distasties" of life. Let's turn to the book of Genesis 3.*

DISCUSSION (OPTION 1: HIS STORY, MY STORY)

Before students begin reading, encourage them to have some time of prayer, reflection, and meditation. Read Genesis 3:1-5 with the group alternating verses—guys reading odd verses, girls even. After the reading, ask something like,

What might Eve have been tempted to think about God's character after listening to the serpent? Why? Have you ever felt that God was distant from your life?

Hand out copies of **His Story, My Story** (page 52) and have students share their stories. Pull out His Story, the timeline of God's most significant events in his relationship to Israel, and have the youth superimpose their sheets within the greater sheet of what God is doing in history.

Possible points of emphasis—

Each person is living out the amazing, eternal, awesome plan of God. As such, there's nothing ordinary about anyone's life. Emphasize how both long-time churched believers from childhood and those who experience dramatic conversions later in life are living in the exciting wave of God's plan.

Pointing to the end of His Story, bring comfort to those students who need comfort about life circumstances on this particular day. Show that throughout history, though there may be "distasties" at different times, God will be faithful to glorify his people.

Encourage people to action. We know what the end will look like: the new heavens and new earth, the presence of God in our midst, and everlasting worship. Since we know the outcome for the future, we can be bold about our lives today.

Ask something like,

How do you think we have a better perspective on life than Eve or most of the people in the Bible?

TRANSITION

Say something like,

Indeed we have a much better perspective on life and God's plan than anyone in Genesis. We have the cross to remind us of God's love, the Holy Spirit to aid us, and each other to encourage us in our walks. We have many blessings in our lives and need to count such blessings regularly. Human hearts get used to the blessings in our lives. Things lose their appeal, and we begin to look more at the blessings rather than the one who blesses.

DISCUSSION (OPTION 2: FOCUS SHIFT)

Hand out copies of **Howard Hughes** (page 53) and say something like,

This is a rather grotesque illustration of what sin can do.

Read the handout together.

Allow students to take a few moments to share some honest wants in their lives and ask kids to say whether they think their wants are bad, good, or neutral.

Hand out copies of **Focus Shift** (page 54) and give kids about 10 minutes to fill out the handout. Ask something like,

What is the one thing that you feel God is not allowing you to have that you think would enhance your life?

Have students label the center tree with that withheld object and the remaining tree text boxes with blessings such as health, shoes, family members, eyes, food, clothing, car, etc. Ask three volunteers to read Genesis 2:8-9, 2:16-17, and 3:2-5 and ask something like—

- *What do we learn about God's character in these verses?*
- *How do you think the serpent wanted to portray God?*

Say something like,

God blesses us with certain things in our lives, and certain things he doesn't allow us to have. But God blesses you in what he gives to you AND in what he withholds from you.

DISCUSSION (OPTION 3: FROM FIG RAGS TO RICHES)

Ask a student volunteer to read Genesis 3:6-19. Ask something like,

What were Adam and Eve's consequences for taking things into their own hands?

(Possible answers include: shame, the curse of labor for Eve, difficulty in work, the serpent cursed to crawl on his stomach, relational difficulties between men and women, and the eventual struggle between humankind and evil.)

Now say something like,

We all make mistakes. What's important afterward is appropriately dealing with the consequences. Notice how God sought Adam and Eve after their disobedience. God sought them out not because he couldn't find them, but because he wanted them to return willingly. Likewise, God seeks us out but also desires for us to return openly.

Ask,

What did Adam and Eve do that showed they weren't being open with God?

Pass out and read **Designer Fig Leaves** (page 55) together. Then ask something like,

Does this true-life college story have any echoes in high school?

Ask students how their schools and perhaps personal lives reflect this.

TRANSITION

Say something like,

In many different ways this story illustrates what happens with our spiritual bodies. Like a marker the Spirit convicts us of sin, but we prefer to cover up his work.

Ask,

According to Genesis 2:14-19 what were the punishments for eating from the tree of the knowledge of good and evil? Did God punish Adam and Eve or did someone else?

TRANSITION

(You can use this after any of the other transitions or discussion options.) Say something like,

"Confession is admitting one's faults, voluntarily coming to God and telling him what he already knows. We are going to have an opportunity right now to come before God."

CLOSING: LEAVES OF FORGIVENESS

Before the meeting prepare enough fig leaf cutouts for your students, along with red paint, bowls to put the paint in, a tarp to cover the floor, nails, and a few hammers. Ahead of time arrange wooden planks in the shape of a cross (to be put out on the floor when you do this activity). Hand out the fig leaf cutouts and have students write their spiritual struggles and sin(s) on the leaves.

On the other side have students write a letter to God telling how they've been dealing with sin. Have they been hiding? Are they responding with anger or bitterness? Ask the students to hold onto their fig leaves.

INTERESTING TIDBIT: FIRST BLOOD (ANOTHER DISCUSSION OPTION)

God said that if anyone ate from the tree of the knowledge of good and evil death would ensue. Yet Adam and Eve did not immediately die. This is striking when we consider that the first death narrated in Genesis is an unspecified animal that was skinned to cover the nakedness and shame of the two perpetrators.

Say something like,

In Genesis 3:21 for God to be able to make a garment of skin for Adam and his wife, an animal had to be killed. In 2 Corinthians 5:21, we find out that Jesus covers our sins with his righteousness. How is this possible? For any animal to be made into a skin garment, blood has to be shed. When Jesus was crucified on the cross, the Bible says that his blood covers our sin. The righteousness of Jesus therefore becomes ours through the cross.

While you lay out a tarp and bring out the wooden cross, play meditative, slow, Christ-centered worship music or hymns in the background and dim the lights.

After a time of reflection ask the youth to dip their fig leaves in the red paint so that the writing is covered and nail the fig leaves to the cross. As students finish, encourage them to pray individually and with others who are finished.

Have a volunteer read this closing prayer: "The love of God covers your sins. He will never leave you nor forsake you. He is the God of Israel and blesses your life with all he gives and all he withholds. Bring your sins to him and receive his forgiveness. Find peace in Jesus Christ, the Lamb of God, who was slain to cover our nakedness. Amen."

Quietly dismiss the group. Remember to take pictures and allow enough time for the paint to dry. Use the cross covered in "blood"-stained fig leaves as a reminder of Jesus' cross.

RUSTY IRON CHEF

Figure out all the ingredients necessary for making a basic meat lasagna. The person with the most correct ingredients wins.

_____

_____

_____

_____

_____

_____

_____

_____

_____

_____

HIS STORY (THIS TIMELINE MARKS THE SIGNIFICANT EVENTS FOR GOD AS WE LOOK IN THIS STORY AND THE END OF TIME.)

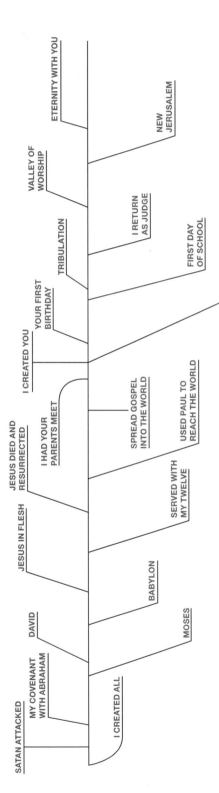

SATAN ATTACKED

MY COVENANT WITH ABRAHAM

DAVID

I CREATED ALL

BABYLON

MOSES

JESUS IN FLESH

JESUS DIED AND RESURRECTED

I HAD YOUR PARENTS MEET

I CREATED YOU

YOUR FIRST BIRTHDAY

SPREAD GOSPEL INTO THE WORLD

SERVED WITH MY TWELVE

USED PAUL TO REACH THE WORLD

TRIBULATION

VALLEY OF WORSHIP

ETERNITY WITH YOU

I RETURN AS JUDGE

FIRST DAY OF SCHOOL

NEW JERUSALEM

MY STORY (ON THIS TIMELINE MARK WHAT YOU FEEL HAVE BEEN THE MOST SIGNIFI-CANT EVENTS IN YOUR LIFE WHETHER GOOD OR BAD.)

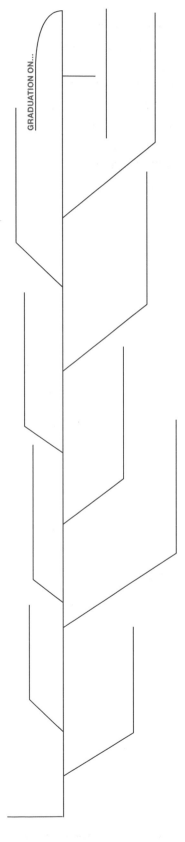

GRADUATION ON...

HOWARD HUGHES

All he really wanted in life was more. He wanted more money, so he parlayed his inherited wealth into a million-dollar pile of assets. He wanted more fame, so he broke into the Hollywood scene and became a filmmaker and star. He wanted more sensual pleasures from women, so he paid handsome sums of money to indulge his every sexual urge. He wanted more thrills, so he designed, built, and piloted the fastest aircraft in the world. He wanted more power, so he secretly dealt political favors so skillfully that two U.S. presidents became his pawns. All he ever really wanted was more. You see, he was absolutely convinced that "more" would bring him happiness.

Unfortunately, history shows otherwise. Here is a brief chronicle of the last days of this man's life:

He was emaciated, practically skeletal, with only 120 pounds stretched over his six-foot, four-inch frame. There was hardly a speck of color anywhere on his body, even in his lips. He was not dead, but his body already seemed to be decaying. Only the long gray hair that trailed halfway down his back, the thin straggly beard that reached midway down his sunken chest, and his hideously long nails that extended several inches in grotesque yellow corkscrews from his fingers and toes seemed to be still growing, still showing signs of life. Then there were his eyes. Near the end of his life they often looked dead and blank, but other times they gleamed from their deep-sunk sockets with surprising, almost frightening intensity. Many of his teeth were rotting black stumps. A tumor was emerging from the side of his head, a reddened lump protruding from his sparse strands of gray hair. His bedsores festered all the way down his back, some so severe that one shoulder bone eventually poked through his parchment-like skin. Then there were his needle marks. The telltale tracks ran the full length of both his thin arms, scarred his thighs, and clustered horribly around his groin. The man's name was Howard Hughes, and he died a billionaire junkie. He banked his whole life on the lie that the unbridled pursuit of more leads to gladness. By reading about the end of his life, we learn that it actually leads to madness.[8]

8 Bill Hybels, *Character: Reclaiming Six Endangered Qualities* (Grand Rapids, MI: Willow Creek Resources, Zondervan Publishing, 1997), 47-48.

FOCUS SHIFT

DESIGNER FIG LEAVES

YOU'LL NEED
- Bibles
- pens/pencils
- copies of **Multimedia** (page 64)
- large sheet of paper
- marker
- small flower pots
- soil
- marigold seeds
- plant flash cards
- gum or candy
- tape
- box
- copies of **A Chronology of Foolishness** (page 65)
- the movie *Day After Tomorrow*
- copies of **Cruel or Just?** (page 66)
- copies of **Role Play: Noah and His Contemporaries** (pages 67-68)

BIG IDEA

Sometimes staying faithful means going against our culture and doing things that may seem illogical or foolish. Noah was living in a time when people went their own way and couldn't give a rip about God. In the midst of this culture God asked Noah to perform a time-consuming, huge, and illogical task. It took sweat...ridicule... suffering...but in the end Noah was vindicated for his righteousness.

OPENER (OPTION 1: MULTIMEDIA)

Say something like,

Let's investigate the overall tone of today's culture and society by looking at what our media portrays and reports. During this exercise you're free to roam around, but make sure you sit back down in 15 minutes.

Give each student a copy of **Multimedia** (page 64) and instruct kids to get into groups of no more than three. Let them know that the questions at the bottom of the sheet will be answered during whole-group discussion.

When the students return, have them share some of their findings. Then ask the following questions and give your students a few moments to fill in the blanks at the bottom of the sheet.

> • *What positive things did you see in the media?*
>
> • *Overall, would you say that the tone of our current culture and society is healthy? or How would you describe the tone of our culture and society?*
>
> • *Where do you think we can find hope in times like these? What do people turn to for hope?*

On a large piece of paper write in big words at the top The World We Live in and write down the main points of the discussion. Jot down both major statements and minor comments.

Ask,

> *What do you think our society should be like, and if it were up to you, what would you change about our society?*

OPENER (OPTION 2: NAME THAT PLANT)

Before the meeting, purchase some small pots (one per student), soil, and marigold flower seeds and keep them in a closed box. Make sure you hide the seed packaging so that no student knows what kind of seed they have. Prepare some flash cards with pictures of common plants (e.g., cactus, rose, dandelion, sunflower, etc.), show each card to the group and have students guess the plants' names, and award candy or gum to the student who shouts out the correct name for each plant first. Tape a marigold seed on one of the flash cards and give kids the opportunity to guess what plant it is without revealing the correct answer. Distribute a few seeds to each student along with soil and a pot from the box. Tell them to write their names and the date on their pots and spend some time planting the seeds (give kids directions from the seed package). As soon as everyone is done planting their seeds, say something like,

> *Okay, look at your pots and wait a few moments. Whoever is able to name what kind of plant it is first gets a special prize* (perhaps a voucher for free ice-cream or a movie ticket).

Wait a few moments. Obviously, the plants will not germinate anytime soon. As students realize that nothing will happen, say something like,

> *The prize stands. Whoever can first identify which plant it is and actually bring the plant to a future group meeting once it has sprouted wins. This means that for the next few days and possibly weeks, you'll have to water the seed, keep it near sunlight, and make sure your pet doesn't eat it. Maybe you can also use the plant*

as a reminder to spend time with God daily—as the seed will need water every day, spend some time with God every day. The point is that living by faith often requires that we remain faithful even when we don't see the final end, and sometimes that final end is a long time coming. Today's lesson is about a person who God put through a similar faith exercise: Noah.

DISCUSSION (OPTION 1: A CHRONOLOGY OF FOOLISHNESS)

Have kids take a paragraph each and read Genesis 6:5-22, underlining anything they find interesting. After they're done reading, ask them the following questions:

• *Why did God decide to send floodwaters upon the earth? Which verses describe this?*

• *Why do you think God wanted to wipe out his creation but preserve Noah and two of every kind of animal?*

Say something like,

Many of you may have heard the story of Noah since you were toddlers: The flood, the animals in the ark, and the rainbow are images many of us know. Today we'll adapt the story to our lives and discuss being a fool for God and the covenant God made with people. Let's begin by reviewing the important events of the account.

Hand out copies of **A Chronology of Foolishness** (page 65). Ask students to pair up and fill in the information.

Here are the answers. *(1. Noah is 500 years old. 2. God explains the reason for the flood. 3. God gives the building instructions. 4. Rain starts when Noah is 600 years, two months, and 17 days old. 5. The rain lasts for 40 days and 40 nights. 6. The animals come and God shuts Noah and the animals in. 7. The flood lasts for 150 days. 8. Dry ground appears. 9. Noah and the animals come out. 10. God gives the covenant in the form of a rainbow.)*

Once kids finish, invite them to share their answers and opinions. After the discussion say something like,

By the way, do you think it was even possible to build such an ark and stock it with all kinds of animals? Listen to what scientists have said about the size of the boat.

Read or summarize for your group the following Interesting Tidbit.

INTERESTING TIDBIT: COULD ALL THE ANIMALS FIT INTO THE ARK?[9]

• Noah could have taken youthful or smaller animals.

• Noah didn't need to take fish or other aquatic creatures on the ark. The dimensions of the ark would comfortably allow the support of all land animals.

• The volume of Noah's ark would have been 1,396,000 cubic feet.

• The gross tonnage of Noah's ark would have been 13,960 tons.

• The capacity of Noah's ark would have been 522 railroad stock cars, which could hold 125,280 sheep-sized animals.

• Because of speciation (i.e., two canines created all the different dog breeds today), only about 16,000 individual animals would've been necessary on Noah's ark.

DISCUSSION (OPTION 2: CRUEL OR JUST?)

Show the clip from *The Day After Tomorrow* where New York City is getting submerged by a huge tidal wave (scene 14, marker 48:06 to 51:12, about three minutes).

Say something like,

There was widespread devastation on earth in the days of Noah. The video clip from The Day After Tomorrow *gives us a visual idea of the magnitude of destruction that nature can unleash.*

Instruct your students to open their Bibles, turn to Genesis 7:17-24, and read together in unison. Ask—

• *How do you think the average person would respond to God after watching this clip and reading this passage?*

• *What would he think about the nature of God?*

Then say something like,

What God did may initially sound rather harsh. But let's not forget that people's hearts were rebellious during that time. Although God created humans for his own glory, humankind turned its back on God. Theologians say it was necessary for God to do this for the sake of humanity and creation. Let's see if we can find out why in the following study.

9 Noah's Ark Search, www.noahsarksearch.com/faq.htm

Hand out copies of **Cruel or Just?** (page 66) and lead your students in reading and discussing the verses listed to answer whether they feel that God was cruel or just. You could also play devil's advocate to help the kids develop their beliefs about God's righteousness.

Read 2 Peter 2:5 together and ask questions like—

- *What title is used to describe Noah?*
- *Why do you suppose Peter gives Noah this title?*
- *What are the good things in Noah's life that we should try to imitate?*
- *In the history of God's work with humankind, why is Noah an important figure?*

Have your students fill in the cruel/just statement after the discussion.

Read 2 Peter 3:1-13 together and ask questions like—

- *What does this passage refer to?*
- *What was society in Noah's time like? Describe that. What do you think society is like today? Describe it.*
- *Describe the people in Simon Peter's day.*
- *According to the verses how should we live? Why?*
- *What will God restore the wicked world with?*

Have your students fill in the cruel/just statement after the discussion. Finally, ask kids to answer the summary question on their sheets and share their answers.

DISCUSSION (OPTION 3: NOAH ROLE PLAY)

This is an organized skit that your students can have fun with while learning. One of the benefits of role playing is that kids get actual practice for possible real-life situations that may come up.

Divide kids into three groups of about equal size. Hand out one copy of **Role Play: Noah and His Contemporaries** (pages 67-68) to each team and assign a different scene to each team. Instruct the groups to be as creative and contemporary as possible. Give the teams about 20 minutes to prepare their skits and tell each team to come up with a "The moral of the story is…" statement to wrap up their presentation with.

When the groups finish preparing, have them come back and present their skits to each other.

TRANSITION

Say something like,

> *The fact is, we may talk about the wickedness of society and the world we live in, but the reality is that all of us to some extent contribute to that wickedness. Believers, though, are spectacularly blessed because we have a covenant with God. A few lessons ago we discovered what the idea of covenant means. In Genesis 9:12-13 the word* covenant *comes up again.*

Ask,

> *What do you remember about covenants? What is a covenant?*

If your students have a hard time remembering, repeat the definition of covenant offered in Session Two.

INTERESTING TIDBIT: A HINT OF WHAT'S TO COME?

Read the following excerpt out loud and explain that the word for "rainbow" and "battle bow" is the same in the Hebrew text. Most important, point out that the bow points up toward God as the target in the case the covenant gets broken.

> The covenant carries the idea of a peace treaty. The enmity that characterized the former relationship between the parties of the covenant is set aside by God's grace. This may be suggested by the fact that the word for 'rainbow' is the usual word for an offensive weapon of war, a battle bow. It is quite possible that the symbolism of the rainbow speaks of the fact that God laid down his weapon of war and thus put away the wrath that had led to the judgment of the flood. In the flood, God's bow was aimed toward the earth in judgment, but once God placed his bow in the sky, the plane of the earth becomes the bowstring and the weapon is now pointed upward toward God, and thus God himself becomes the recipient of the threatened covenant curse. It would be nice to find a...reference to Christ in the rainbow—the bow is aimed, as it were, toward the cross, where God takes the curse of the covenant upon himself.[10]

Ask something like,

> *With all the sins that we personally commit, we can be comforted to know that God won't wipe us out as in the days of Noah. According to the excerpt, why do you*

think that Christians can be especially thankful? (God took upon himself the punishment for our sins. On the cross Jesus became the slaughtered Lamb of God.)

CLOSING

Let your group know that you'll be going into a time of prayer. Have the kids sit in a circle. Ask for volunteers to share their temptations and the difficulties they have living in today's society.

As each volunteer finishes sharing, invite him or her to kneel in the middle of the circle. Ask for the others to gather close (if they're comfortable, have them lay hands on the volunteer) and pray that like Noah, he or she will become "faithful and a preacher of righteousness."

End the meeting by reading from Revelation 21:1-4.

MULTIMEDIA

You have 15 minutes to come up with and/or examine five different kinds of secular, general public media, such as magazines, current hit movies, current hit songs, current newspapers, and current TV shows.

- If it's a written medium (magazine or newspaper), write down the major headlines or sections you find on the first page.

- If you choose TV, watch for about 10 minutes, flipping through the major channels (not specialty channels).

- If you choose a movie, name the title.

- In the middle column write a brief summary of what that publication, show, or movie is about.

- In the right column describe what each medium reveals about society.

One example is given.

TYPE OF MEDIA	BRIEF SUMMARY	WHAT IT REVEALS ABOUT SOCIETY
News show	There is violent protesting and civil unrest due to a change in government in the Middle East	Violence Disunity Strong opinions People are not at peace with each other.

WRAP-UP

Positive things I see:

Overall, the tone of our culture is_____.

In today's world I believe people find hope and turn to _____.

A CHRONOLOGY OF FOOLISHNESS

WHAT DO THESE VERSES SAY? (PUT IN YOUR OWN WORDS.)

1. Genesis 5:32 _____

2. Genesis 6:5-8 _____

3. Genesis 6:14-18 _____

4. Genesis 7:11 _____

5. Genesis 7:12 _____

6. Genesis 7:15-16 _____

7. Genesis 7:24 _____

8. Genesis 8:13,14 _____

9. Genesis 8:18,19 _____

10. Genesis 9:12-16 _____

WHAT THE VERSES DON'T SAY (BUT WHAT WE CAN GUESS!)

FAITH OVER TIME

• According to Genesis 5:32 and 7:6, at least how long did it take to build the ark?

• What might Noah also have been doing while building? (Check out 2 Peter 2:5.)

FAITH DESPITE PUBLIC OPINION

• What kind of conversations do you think may've taken place between Noah and onlookers?

• How do you think people reacted when they saw animals come together and line up in front of the ark?

FAITH AND EFFORT

• What kind of sins do you think Noah kept himself from that other people were indulging in?

• List some challenges that might've gone along with building the ark and supplying it with food for all the animals.

21ST-CENTURY NOAH

• What kind of things that the Bible calls sin are rather common in your school?

• What are some of the temptations that you face every day?

CRUEL OR JUST?

In this exercise we'll try to see the justice in an act that most people would say was cruel (the flood). We'll read the verses together. Don't fill in the blanks until after the group discussion of each passage. When we finish discussing, write a response and indicate why you think God was cruel or just.

FROM 2 PETER 2:5

I believe God is (cruel/ just) _____ because _____

_____

_____

_____

_____

_____

FROM 2 PETER 3:1-13

I believe God is (cruel/ just) _____ because _____

_____

_____

_____

_____

_____

SUMMARY

What does the study of Noah's life teach us about God and about human beings?

_____

_____

_____

_____

_____

_____

ROLE PLAY: NOAH AND HIS CONTEMPORARIES

YOUR MISSION: PREPARE A SKIT ABOUT PART OF NOAH'S STORY.

RULES:
• Your leader will assign a different scene to each group.
• Be as creative and as contemporary as possible.
• Use as many props as you can find.
• At the bottom of your scene is a statement you have to think about and complete as a group.
• You have 20 minutes to prepare. Then be ready to present your skit and statement to the other groups.

SCENE 1: TEMPTATION
• Consider that some of the wicked people may have been Noah's friends or contemporaries.
• What were some sins you think the people indulged in?
• Imagine the sins that Noah had to resist and the temptations he had to face.
• Now come up with a scene with these same elements but relevant to a typical day in your high school.

When you are finished practicing, complete this statement.
The moral of the story is _____

_____

_____

SCENE 2: CRAZY IDEAS
• Imagine God's conversation with Noah concerning the building instructions for the ark.
• Imagine Noah explaining the incredible task to one of his contemporary friends before he's done any of the construction.
• Think about Noah preaching righteousness to his friend and imagine his friend's reaction.
• Now creatively replay these situations or make a similar skit that could actually happen with one of your nonbelieving friends.

When you are finished practicing, complete this statement.
The moral of the story is _____

_____

_____

SCENE 3: NOAH'S STEADFASTNESS (50 YEARS LATER)

• Consider what kind of perseverance Noah needed to build the ark. Think about Noah sharing his progress 50 years later with his same old group of friends, highlighting Noah's confidence in God. (How long did it take to build the ark?)

• Imagine the friends asking questions about lodging room for all the animals, keeping the ark clean once built, and finding food for all the animals.

• Act this scene out using modern language and ideas and reenact how you might show your confidence in God during trials or tough times.

When you are finished practicing, complete this statement.

The moral of the story is _____

_____

_____

BIG IDEA

What is God's agenda for ethnic unity and diversity? By looking at God's intervention in the Tower of Babel and Abraham's life, this lesson will teach a biblical understanding of unity, ethnic diversity, and God's plan of redeemed worship for all nations.

OPENER (OPTION 1: CHOPSTICK RACE)

Before the meeting purchase a pack of chopsticks (about 100 pairs) and divide them into two bundles. Take one bundle of 48 pairs of chopsticks and tape it together: eight pairs per layer, six layers high. Make sure the bundle is tightly packed together. Take the remaining 48 pairs of chopsticks and break up the pairs so that you have 96 individual sticks.

During the meeting announce the impending race of speed and strength and ask for two volunteers. Make sure one of the volunteers is considerably smaller than the other one (having a guy race a girl works best) and explain that the race will consist of who can break 96 chopsticks first.

YOU'LL NEED

- Bibles
- pens/pencils
- 100 pairs of chopsticks
- tape
- a large white bedsheet
- permanent markers
- paint
- index cards
- boxes of angel hair pasta
- bags of mini-marshmallows
- copies of **Leaning Tower of Babel** (page 74)
- copies of **Past, Present, and Future** (page 75)
- poster board
- recordings of worship music from around the world

From Genesis 1 to Revelation 22, the Bible is a story of God's creation and his relationship to humankind. The recurrent themes of Scripture are God's blessing, people's disobedience, God's displeasure, some kind of payment or sacrifice to atone for sin, and God's blessing again. The cycle repeats until the appearance of Jesus promised through Genesis 3 and the covenants, beginning with the Abrahamic covenant. Christ breaks the cycle of blessing and sin, and God's people are reconciled with God once and for all, through faith by grace. Particularly important: The modern believer's story of faith also mirrors the greater story of the history of Israel, from slavery to sin en route to a promised land.

The question we want to answer is, "How does the Tower of Babel account fit into the main story between

continued next page

Hand the bundled set to the stronger of the two. Hand the 96 individual sticks to the smaller or weaker contestant. When both contestants are ready, count down from three and start. If the bundling is done well, the set should not break. The individual sticks will be broken first.

Give the students an opportunity to think about what the exercise demonstrated by saying something like,

What do you think this illustrates?

Then say something like,

This simply shows that there's strength in unity.

As an option, point out that in Genesis 3 the serpent asks Eve about the tree of knowledge of good and evil when the direction to safeguard the tree was given to Adam.

Ask the students something like,

Do you guys have people in your life who strengthen and encourage you when you're with them?

OPENER (OPTION 2: THE BEAUTY OF COLORS)

Prior to the meeting prepare on a large white bedsheet a simple design of a cross or other Christian symbol with a permanent marker. Make these lines thick. Add a number of designs on the white sheet with thinner lines corresponding to the size of your group (maybe one design per every three kids). The final product should look somewhat like a large puzzle. Cut up the sheet into a few sections and make sure that the edges don't fray.

When your group gets together, hand out different sections to different small groups of students and ask them to color the sheet, changing colors between design lines. Make sure they can't see what the original image looked like. Have groups use markers, paint, or any other coloring medium that stays on cloth and dries quickly.

When they're done, ask the students to rejoin the larger group with their colored sections. In a larger area (e.g., on the floor) connect the pieces back together (you could eventually sew them together) and sit around the finished product.

Ask something like,

As you look at the final product, what do you think we can learn about how God made people in the world different?

OPENER (OPTION 3: SHARING)

Gather your group in a circle to begin a discussion of race relations and Christianity. Beforehand write down the following four questions on a few index cards, and if your group is large enough, divide into smaller groups. Ask students to share their answers to the questions and then be ready for a discussion.

The four questions are:

• WHAT IS THE ETHNIC MAKEUP OF YOUR SCHOOL—WHAT PERCENTAGE IS CAUCASIAN, AFRICAN AMERICAN, HISPANIC, ASIAN, ETC.?

• HOW DO DIFFERENT ETHNIC GROUPS IN YOUR SCHOOL GENERALLY TREAT EACH OTHER? WOULD YOU SAY THAT THERE IS ANY RACIAL TENSION? EXPLAIN OR GIVE EXAMPLES.

• DOES OUR CHURCH HAVE A SPECIFIC ETHNIC MAJORITY? IF SO, HOW DO YOU THINK PEOPLE FROM OTHER ETHNIC GROUPS MAY FEEL ABOUT COMING TO OUR MINISTRY?

• WHAT COULD YOU DO TO MAKE THOSE OF DIFFERENT ETHNIC GROUPS FEEL MORE WELCOME IN OUR MINISTRY?

When you regather as a large group, ask small groups to share their answers.

DISCUSSION (OPTION 1: LEANING TOWER OF BABEL)

Before the meeting buy boxes of angel hair pasta and bags of mini-marshmallows. Make sure you have a level, flat area to work on. Tables work best. The best team size will be four to five students. One box of pasta will provide enough building material for three teams. (Beware of students dropping marshmallows on the ground and stepping on them.) Put on some background music as you see fit but make sure to play it rather quietly. For this exercise students will not be allowed to speak; the only means of communication will be body language.

Read Genesis 11:1-9 together. Before the activity say something like,

Today's activity consists of building the highest possible tower, similar to what we just read about in Genesis 11. You will be divided into different teams, and whoever builds the highest structure in 25 minutes wins. Be aware that time flies. The construction materials will be spaghetti and marshmallows. However, there's a catch. Nobody is allowed to talk or speak to one another. You can only use body language to communicate!

Break kids into groups of four or five, hand out copies of **Leaning Tower of Babel** (page 74), and give groups about 25 minutes to build their structures. After time is up, ask the students to remain in their groups and go through the rest of the worksheet (they can talk now).

Theological Tidbit cont.

the Noah and Abraham accounts in Genesis 9 and 12?"

We find an answer when we remember that after the flood, God blesses Noah and his sons in Genesis 9:1 and instructs them to be "fruitful and increase in number and fill the earth." God explains how murder is evil based on the foundation that all humans are image bearers of God. In Genesis 10 we read that Noah's children, Shem, Ham and Japheth, are the source for all the nations that eventually spread over the earth (v. 32). We discover in Genesis 11 that due to a common ancestry, "the whole world had one language and a common speech" (v. 1), but in disobedience to God's blessing and calling to subdue the earth and spread (see **The Cultural Mandate** later), God's people gather on the plain on Shinar (v. 2) and begin building the Tower of Babel (v. 4). God's people rebel and sin against God. The result is that God confuses the languages of the people and scatters them over the earth (v. 9).

continued next page

Abram's call in Genesis 12 is therefore the answer to the ongoing disobedience and sin described in Genesis 3 through 11. The table of nations and the Tower of Babel are a prologue to the call and promise given to Abraham.

Genesis 12:2-3 introduces God's spectacular redemptive plan that culminates in Jesus Christ himself. Although people repeatedly sin against God and each other, God makes a covenant with Abraham that eventually results in a Savior and a nation of worshipers from all the peoples of earth.

Within the covenant with Abraham part of God's redemptive plan as revealed in Genesis is to save and bless individuals from all peoples of the earth and to reunite them as the people of God. Therefore, racial divisions in the church and racial segregation among the people of God move away from following God's redemptive plan.

While students answer the questions on the handout, determine which team built the highest structure.

Once students finish the handout, gather the whole group together and go through the questions, discussing any points of interest. After the last discussion question award the winner of the competition with—you guessed it—pasta and marshmallows. For a twist use different types of pasta and different sized marshmallows.

DISCUSSION (OPTION 2: PAST, PRESENT, AND FUTURE)

Divide your students into groups of three to four and hand out copies of **Past, Present, and Future** (page 75). Assign a different section to each group and give them about 25 minutes to find the answers. When they're done, ask a volunteer from each group to give a brief summary of their answers, then go over the group discussion point at the bottom of the sheet.

Be prepared with a marker and poster board to jot down the major points of the discussion and the major ways this text can be applied.

TRANSITION

Say something like,

> *Now that we've discovered the meaning of the Tower of Babel and God's promise to Abraham, let's think about the fact that when Jesus was crucified, they fastened a notice to the cross that read, "Jesus of Nazareth, the King of the Jews" in Latin, Aramaic, and Greek, the major languages of that period. Let's use the remainder of the time to make some commitments.*

CLOSING (OPTION 1: WORSHIP FROM THE WORLD)

Prior to the meeting gather worship music from around the world. Worship songs in Spanish, Korean, German, and French are readily available on the Internet. Ask a student to read from John 17:20-23 while there is music playing the background.

Close the meeting by asking students to sit in a circle and pray together. Ask students to pray for the following:

- Unity among all believers in your community regardless of ethnicity
- That your church would develop a deeper vision to love people of all ethnicities

- Personal repentance for prejudice or ethnic sin
- Personal commitment to love all people since they are made in the image of God

End the prayer meeting by reading from Revelation 22:12-16.

CLOSING (OPTION 2: IBMS (INTERNATIONAL BIBLE MEMORIES))

At the end of the meeting hand out index cards with John 3:16 written on one side in English. Ask students to find a translation of John 3:16 in a foreign language of their choosing, preferably corresponding to a language one of their friends speaks. Ask kids to ask their friends for a colloquial translation. Tell your students to use this as a potential evangelism opportunity or just a way to get to know someone better.

As a variation prepare the John 3:16 verses in a few languages before the meeting and ask students to memorize the verse of their choice in one of the other languages.

THE CULTURAL MANDATE

"The cultural mandate" refers to the Christian calling to live actively in society, have dominion over nature, and impact world cultures to the glory of God. The cultural mandate assumes that according to Genesis 1:26-28, God's people should spread out and fill the earth, therefore making God known everywhere. Although we're called to redeem culture, take care of the poor, and rescue the underprivileged, our primary calling is, however, spiritual in nature and relies on the power of the gospel message to change hearts and renew minds.

LEANING TOWER OF BABEL

RULES

- You have a 25-minute time limit.
- Use only the building materials provided.
- During the activity nobody is allowed to talk. The only acceptable means of communication is body language.

BUILDING PLAN (NO SPEECH, NO WRITING, ONLY DRAWING)

DISCUSS

1. What was easy or hard about this exercise?

2. How did the language restriction impact your ability to build?

FROM GENESIS 11:1-9

1. According to these verses what were the improved building materials people used for construction?

2. God confused languages and scattered people over the face of the whole earth. What results do you think this may have caused in history?

FAST-FORWARD TO THE NEW TESTAMENT

1. Read Acts 2:1-13. Why do you think God allowed these people to speak in languages not their own?

2. Read Revelation 7:9-10. What does the church at the end of time look like?

3. In light of Revelation 7:9-10 what do you think one possible calling of the modern-day church might be?

PAST, PRESENT, AND FUTURE

As a team answer the questions in the section assigned to you by your leader. Take about 15 minutes. When you finish, pick a volunteer to give a brief summary of your answers and be ready to go over the group discussion point at the bottom of the sheet.

READ GENESIS 1 AND OTHER VERSES LISTED.

1. Read Genesis 1:26-27. According to the text what unifies humanity?

2. What are the common themes of Genesis 1:28, Genesis 9:1-3, Genesis 11:8, and Genesis 12:1-3?

3. What do you think it means to subdue the earth?

4. In what ways can God's people subdue the earth? Give some examples.

READ GENESIS 10-11:4.

1. After the flood which groups of people began to spread over the earth (Genesis 10:32)? Who were they?

2. According to Genesis 11 how many languages did the world initially have?

3. What did the people use to build the Tower of Babel?

4. Why did the people want to build a tower?

5. Can you think of any modern Towers of Babel? Explain your reasoning.

READ GENESIS 1:26-28 AND 11:5-9.

1. According to Genesis 1:26-28 what should have God's people been doing?

2. Why did God oppose the building?

3. How did God stop the construction plan?

4. Why do you think God scattered the people?

READ GENESIS 11:1-9, ACTS 2:1-13, AND REVELATION 7:9-10.

1. What similarities do you see between these verses and Genesis 11:1-9?

2. What differences do you see between these verses and Genesis 11:1-9?

3. According to the two New Testament texts, why do you think God enabled people to speak in different languages?

4. What do you think Revelation 7:9-10 reveals about God's plan for his people?

GROUP DISCUSSION QUESTION

In which ways, if at all, should the prophecy of Revelation 7:9-10 affect today's church and believers?

BIG IDEA

Faith is trusting God and taking risks despite what situations may look like. In this lesson students will learn that God understands our doubts and has given us the ultimate proof of his faithfulness. Though Abraham was not told where to go, he went. Though both he and his wife were old, God eventually blessed them with a family.

OPENER (OPTION 1: TUG OF FAITH)

Ask kids to divide into two groups: people who consider themselves logical thinkers and people who are creative and imaginative. Name the two teams the "Logics" and the "Dreamers." Tell them to make two lines facing each other as they'll be playing tug of war. Allow them to organize their lines as they wish.

Tell kids that after each pull one student will switch teams, leaving his/her side and joining the other side, as determined by a drawing of random index cards that say either "one from Team Dreamers to Team Logic" or "one from Team Logic to Team

YOU'LL NEED
- Bibles
- pens/pencils
- index cards
- offering basket/hat
- rope
- small cups of grape juice
- pieces of bread
- recording of slow prayer music
- copies of **Survivor** (page 83)
- copies of **Abraham's Life: Zipped File** (page 84)
- copies of **Father of Millions** (page 85)
- copies of **Holy Promise** (page 86)

Dreamers." The switching of students must always include one of the stronger kids, maybe the last in their row (sometimes called the anchor).

After the first match draw a card (from an offering basket, hat, etc.). Make sure to make it suspenseful and allow a student to switch sides. Play tug of war again and record who wins.

At the end of each match do another drawing and allow another student to switch sides. Repeat this process as many times as you see fit. After the exercise allow students to cool off as you regroup.

TRANSITION

Read the following quote from C. S. Lewis's *Mere Christianity*.

It is not reason that is taking away my faith: on the contrary, my faith is based on reason. It is my imagination and emotions [that is taking away my faith]. The battle is between faith and reason on one side and emotion and imagination on the other.

Say something like,

This exercise illustrates how we can grow in our faith. Whenever we are going back and forth in making a decision to trust God or not, God calls us to ground ourselves in who he is. There's tension between logic and dreaming. Living by faith is not about random choices but about trusting what we know about God's character, promises, and sacrifice. Today we'll learn how to grow in our faith by looking at Abraham's example in Genesis.

OPENER (OPTION 2: CAN YOU HEAR IT NOW?)

Begin by saying that in the room, you and your students are in the midst of thousands of people singing and talking and music blaring. Obviously, however, your room may be quite still.

Perhaps you can joke around with your students and ask them whether they can "hear it now" (a play on the famous cell phone slogan). Tell them that right in their midst the song _____ (pick one that is constantly aired) and its singer are with them. As the students wonder whether you have lost your marbles, pull out a radio, plug it in, turn it on to FM or AM and scan back and forth between stations, pausing and playing whatever comes up for a few moments. Say something like,

You see—music and voices are always around us, but many times we don't tune

in. Sometimes we don't plug in. Sometimes we don't extend our antennas to catch the music that's always around us. Likewise, living by faith in God requires that we plug in, tune in, and listen to what God has to say. Perhaps we can start this lesson by doing just that. Let's spend some time in prayer.

OPENER (OPTION 3: SURVIVOR)

Hand out copies of **Survivor** (page 83) and have kids read the directions. Then say something like,

Whatever you place in your bag will determine how long you will be able to survive. After you have finished making your packing lists, we'll have an opportunity to share why we picked the listed items. Since the plane you are on is already nose-diving into the Pacific, you have five minutes to pack. Go!

After your students are done, ask volunteers to share why they packed as they did.

TRANSITION

Say something like,

Just as we would need physical items to survive in a physically deserted place, what do you think you would need to survive in a spiritually deserted land? A Bible? Sermons? Your youth group? Today we are going to look at someone who survived and did very well when he had no church, Bible, retreats, or conferences. We are going to look at someone who only had God himself and nothing else. We are going to study Abraham.

TRANSITION: FURTHER OPTION

At this point if your students are not too familiar with the life of Abraham, distribute copies of **Abraham's Life: Zipped File** (page 84) to give them a quick overview of his life. Some Bible passages are included as references and may be used to supplement the summary.

DISCUSSION (OPTION 1: FATHER OF MILLIONS)

Invite your youth to break up into groups of three or four. Hand out copies of **Father of Millions** (page 85) and assign a different chapter to each small group. Tell each team to read the assigned chapters twice: once out loud as a group and then once individually.

For each of the sections lead the discussion by asking questions similar to the following:

GENESIS 12

1. What does Abram have to leave behind to obey God's call?
2. What does God promise Abram in return?
3. Have you ever experienced having to leave something behind in return for a greater promise from God?
4. In verses 10-20 why does Abram think it best to lie concerning his relationship with Sarai?
5. It's strange. Abram lies to Pharaoh even though God has promised him safety wherever he goes. Regardless of Abram's sin, he still comes out on top and leaves Egypt with incredible wealth. What does this tell you about God?
6. Is lying ever justified if it can protect someone you love? Is that kind of lying a sign of lack of faith in God?

GENESIS 15

1. God seems to repeat his covenant promise several times (Genesis 13:14-15, 15:5, 17:6-8). Why do you think God had to do this?
2. What was the promise of God?
3. In a covenant both parties were expected to walk through the slaughtered animals. In this passage who walks in between?
4. Why is it significant that only God walks through the slaughtered animals?
5. What does God do when Abram asks God for reassurance?
6. Jesus Christ calls the last supper a "new covenant." How does the story of the cross resemble the story in Genesis 15?
7. What does the cross of Christ guarantee?

GENESIS 17

1. For what natural reasons does Abraham doubt God?
2. What does this tell you concerning faith?
3. How old are Abraham and Sarah when they become parents?
4. What seemingly impossible situation are you facing today that you doubt God can have any impact on? How have you tried to take things into your own hands?

Be ready to jot down anything interesting on a poster or marker board for the whole group to discuss later on.

DISCUSSION (OPTION 2: HOLY PROMISE)

Read Genesis 15 together as a group. Have different students read different paragraphs. Say something like,

> *Abram is so much like you and me. God has promised him incredible blessings. And although Abram believes God's promise in verses 5 and 6, he also wants some kind of proof. Amazingly, the Lord proves his trustworthiness to Abram and makes a covenant with him. Let's find out what this means.*

Hand out copies of **Holy Promise** (page 86) to your students and go through the worksheet. Go over the What's Going on in Genesis 15? section and then have the kids organize themselves and reenact the covenant. Give them enough time to answer the questions listed in the handout. Finally, go over what they came up with to fill in the last statement.

TRANSITION

Say something like,

> *When God does not seem close, or when you doubt God because of logic or imagination or fear that you won't be able to survive, God asks us to look at the cross. On the cross Jesus became the slaughtered Lamb of God because of our shortcomings and lack of trust in him. As we close for today, let's make that personal and apply it.*

CLOSING (OPTION 1: SOLEMN COMMUNITY LOVE FEAST)

Note: Before you go through with this option, make sure that it does not break any constitutional laws of your denomination. This closing option may be repeated with other lessons to reinforce community.

On a separate table prepare small cups of grape juice and pieces of bread. Have slow prayer music playing in the background. Ask students to come up and take a small cup of grape juice and a small piece of bread and stay quiet.

Continue by saying,

> *When we doubt God like Abraham, God doesn't become less faithful. Take some time to walk around and share whatever doubts and trials you may be experiencing with a few brothers and sisters. As each of you finishes sharing, the other person is to break a piece of bread and say, "Look to Jesus who was broken for you." Then*

dip the bread in juice and say, "God reminds us today of his promise to you. Rejoice in the Lord!" Then the other person should have a turn.

Instruct students that this is not communion but a New Testament version of Genesis 15. Ask your students to end their time by praying for each other.

CLOSING (OPTION 2: MEMORY VERSE AND APPLICATION)

Before dismissing your students, hand out index cards and ask students to write down Hebrews 12:2-3 on one side. On the other side ask students to complete the following statement with a personal temptation, problem, or trial.

Because of Jesus, I know God will bless me even though I am_____.

Ask students to keep the verse in a visible location throughout the week and memorize the passage for the next meeting.

SURVIVOR

Imagine you are going to be stranded on a deserted island in the middle of nowhere. What items would you bring to make sure you survive? You'll have no electricity, no cell phone signal, and no volleyball named Wilson. The items you list need to be limited to surviving on the island and may not be used either to contact the outside world or to escape the island. Fill in the following table according to the number of items allowed. By the way, each item must be able to fit in a backpack. Happy surviving!

If I could bring the following number of items, I would bring...

SEVEN ITEMS	FIVE ITEMS	THREE ITEMS	ONE ITEM

Explain your choices to the group.

ABRAHAM'S LIFE: ZIPPED FILE

In Genesis 12:1-7 we discover God's call and promise to Abraham. His and Sarah's original names were Abram and Sarai, and they came from Ur of the Chaldeans. God tells Abram to leave his country and people and go to an unspecified place where God will make him into a great nation. Abram and Sarai, along with Abram's nephew Lot, therefore leave and travel to Canaan, the Promised Land.

God reaffirms his covenant to Abram on several occasions (Genesis 13:14-17, 15:5, and 17:6-8), but Abram and Sarai don't quite know how God will fulfill his promise, especially because Sarai is barren—unable to have children (11:30).

At times they try to take things into their own hands. A severe famine forces Abram and Sarai to go down to Egypt, and because Sarai is beautiful and Abram is afraid, he devises a plan to deceive the Egyptians and conceal their marriage, claiming that they're only brother and sister. Pharaoh takes Sarai as his own and treats Abram with incredible wealth, but as the Lord inflicts diseases on Pharaoh and his household (12:10-20), Pharaoh figures out the truth and releases Abram and Sarai—still with the wealth Abram has acquired in the meantime.

Due to their large flocks and limited land, Lot and Abram part ways near Bethel. Lot settles in Jordan while Abram takes the land of Canaan.

In Genesis 15 God establishes a covenant and promises Abram a great family despite the fact that Sarai is barren. In a moment of doubt Sarai invites Abram to have children through their servant Hagar (16:1-2) who gives birth to Ishmael.

Sarah (both her name and her husband's name change in 17:5 and 17:15) then gets pregnant by Abraham at the age of 91 (17:17, 21) and gives birth to Isaac.

In the New Testament Abraham is recognized as a man who believed God's promises despite circumstances. Truth be told, we discover that he and Sarah were not always confident. Although they sometimes doubted God, God was faithful. Over time they grew in faith and developed an incredible trust in God, even to the point of almost sacrificing Isaac, the one through whom God promised a great legacy.

FATHER OF MILLIONS

Review the chapter assigned to you by reading the chapter twice: once out loud as a group and once individually. Following your group leader's questions, make some notes on what you think the most important elements of the following chapters are.

GENESIS 12

GENESIS 15

GENESIS 17

HOLY PROMISE

WHAT'S GOING ON IN GENESIS 15?

A fundamental element of ancient Near Eastern covenant treaties was the blood oath. A covenant treaty was a solemn promise of peace (between two parties) confirmed by oath and sealed with a bloody sacrifice. In the typical covenant "cutting" ceremony the two sides sacrificed an animal and laid out its dismembered pieces in two parallel lines, creating an aisle between the pieces. Then the parties to the treaty would walk the length of the aisle, enacting their oath, saying, in effect, "May I become like these animals if I do not keep my word with you." (Since the pledge called down a penalty on themselves for failure to keep the covenant, it was called a "self-maledictory oath."[11])

ANSWER THE FOLLOWING QUESTIONS USING GENESIS 15 AS A REFERENCE

1. Rewrite word for word what God promises Abram in verses 4-5 and 12-16.
2. How does Abram respond to God's promise of countless offspring?
3. How many parties walk through the dismembered animals? How many parties should have walked through the dismembered animals?
4. According to What's Going on in Genesis 15 above, why is it significant that only God walks through the animals?

TURN TO AND READ HEBREWS 9:15-20 AND 10:5-10

According to Hebrews what did Jesus become?

READ THE FOLLOWING

"The pleading voice of the patriarch had urged: 'How can I *know*? How can I be sure?' The solemn ceremony of covenantal self-malediction provides the Lord's reply: 'I promise. I solemnly commit myself as almighty God. Death may be necessary. But the promises of the covenant shall be fulfilled.' In Jesus Christ God fulfills his promise. In him God is with us. He offers his own body and his own blood as victim of the covenantal curses. His flesh is torn so that God's word to the patriarch might be fulfilled. Now he offers himself to you. He says: 'Take, eat; this is my body. This is my blood of the covenant shed for many. Drink, all of you, of it.'"[12]

READ HEBREWS 12:2-3 AND FINISH THE FOLLOWING STATEMENT

When Abram wants reassurance, God makes a covenant with him. When Christians now need reassurance, they can...

11 Michael D. Williams, *Far As the Curse Is Found: The Covenant Story of Redemption* (Phillipsburg, NJ: P & R Publishing, 2005), 97-98.
12 O. Palmer Robertson, *Christ of the Covenants* (Phillipsburg, NJ: P & R Publishing, 1981), 146.

ABRAHAM SACRIFICES ISAAC

BIG IDEA

Throughout our lives God may call us to trust in him and make sacrifices. A sacrifice might be breaking up with a girlfriend or taking a semester off before college to go do mission work. For others it may be choosing not to participate in sport competitions on Sundays due to time conflicts with Sunday worship. This lesson will teach the discipline of sacrifice by looking at perhaps the most vivid (second to the cross) example of sacrifice in the Bible: the Abraham and Isaac account.

OPENER (OPTION 1: FAITHFUL INDIANA)

Rent the movie *Indiana Jones and the Last Crusade*. Introduce the film clip by saying something like,

> *Stepping out in faith often means that there may be fearful consequences or losses. As you look at this clip, ask yourself whether God has ever placed you in a similar situation.*

YOU'LL NEED

- Bibles
- pens/pencils
- the movie *Indiana Jones and the Last Crusade*
- index cards
- recording of the song "Enough" by Chris Tomlin
- PowerPoint software
- copies of **Lift by Faith, Not by Sight** (pages 92-93)
- copies of **Lessons in Sacrifice** (page 94)
- copies of **A Series of Unfortunate Events** (page 95)
- copies of **God's Isaac** (page 96)

Start the clip at scene 33, marker 1:47:05, right when Indiana Jones is looking over the chasm, and end it when he throws sand over the hidden bridge to make it visible, marker 1:48:56 (about two minutes).

Begin the discussion by asking the following questions:

- *What was Indiana's act of faith?*
- *What possible losses do you think he might've been thinking about? Gains?*
- *What motivated him to step out in faith?*
- *Can you remember a time when you felt God was calling you to a leap of faith? What were you scared of losing?*

OPENER (OPTION 2: LIFT BY FAITH NOT BY SIGHT)

After greeting your students, ask whether all of them know what pole-vaulting is. As vividly as you can, describe what a pole-vaulter does and hand out copies of **Lift by Faith, Not by Sight** (pages 92-93).

Ask kids to come up with six worst-case scenarios that could happen in the sport of pole-vaulting and see who comes up with the most painful. Then take turns reading the true story so that everyone gets a chance to read. When you get to the end of the story, finish by saying,

> *It is simply because Michael Stone is blind!*

Discuss the two questions at the bottom of the handout.

TRANSITION

Say something like,

> *People who are able to make leaps of faith usually base their faith on some solid truths. Indiana Jones had a little survival manual for the task; Michael Stone had years of training and experience* (depending on the opener you used). *Today we're going to look at one of the most memorable acts of faith in Scripture: God's testing of Abraham by asking Abraham to sacrifice his only son, Isaac. We will discover that Abraham had some solid reasons for trusting God...but regardless, the test must've been gut-wrenching because Abraham loved his only son but was asked to sacrifice him as an offering to God. This lesson will teach us the kind of faith Abraham must have had to be able to do this.*

DISCUSSION (OPTION 1: LESSONS IN SACRIFICE)

Break kids into groups of three or four and hand out **Lessons in Sacrifice** (page 94). Have each small group take on a different section and give kids 15 minutes or so to complete the questions. When 15 minutes are up, have the small groups share their answers with everyone. When each group is done giving answers for their set of questions, ask something like, **What is the core truth that you learned by answering your set of questions?**

DISCUSSION (OPTION 2: A SERIES OF UNFORTUNATE EVENTS)

Pass out the sheet **A Series of Unfortunate Events** (page 95). Say,

God has blessed us in different ways. Make a list of what you feel are the five most important physical things God has blessed you with. (Some possible examples may be parents, an MP3 player, a girlfriend or boyfriend, a computer, a laptop, grades, looks, athletic ability, or their best friends.) Ask kids to be as specific as possible.

After they have completed their lists, let them know that an unfortunate event has happened, and as a result they lost and have to delete one of the items from the list. Tell them that they have a choice as to which item they lose.

With four remaining items let them know that a natural disaster strikes their community, and another of the remaining items of their choice is gone. If it's a dog, it's been sucked up by a tornado. If it's a laptop, it's underwater. If it's a loved one, a stampede of alligators has crushed him to oblivion. Allow them some time to think and cross out one item.

With three remaining items tell the kids that a virus (computer or real) has infected their third item, and it must now be quarantined forever. Again they have a choice of the remaining three items. Have your students delete another one.

You guessed it. Come up with another creative unfortunate event and let your students choose which item they'll give up next. Now have kids share what the item is and what it means to them by saying,

Imagine God now comes to you after all these unfortunate losses and asks you to give up the last item on your sheet. How would you feel if God asked you to give that up?

Have students write down words that describe their feelings toward God on the right-hand side of the handout. Give the students an opportunity to answer the two questions below the boxes and then share their answers. Read the quote from C. S. Lewis together and help students understand its meaning by discussing the questions provided.

INTERESTING TIBIT: OPTION FOR LEADER TEXT

According to the Dictionary of the Old Testament, "The offerer normally slaughtered the animal...and the distinctive nature of the burnt offering was that the whole animal was offered on the altar, the only exceptions being the removal of the hide of the larger animals as part of the slaughtering process."*

* R. E. Averbeck, Dictionary of the Old Testament: Pentateuch, ed. David W. Baker (Downers Grove, IL: InterVarsity Press, 2003), 713.

Now have everyone turn to Genesis 22 and read the text together. When you finish reading, ask the following questions:

> • *One of the reasons Abraham's test puzzles him is because God had promised great blessings through Isaac in Genesis 15:4-5. Usually, those things we have difficulty giving up to God hold some kind of promise to us. What did each of your five items promise you? Share.*
>
> • *Why do you suppose God asks Abraham to give up Isaac?*
>
> • *Why do you suppose God sometimes asks for—or downright takes—something from us?*
>
> • *In Genesis 22:14 we read that God was going to provide at that place, and indeed centuries later Mt. Moriah became Jerusalem, the place where God sacrificed his Son Jesus. What do you think God is saying through this connection?*
>
> • *Let's read Romans 8:32. How does this passage help you trust God when you feel that he is asking you to give up something too big?*

CLOSING (OPTION 1: DUO PRAYER)

Allow the students to end with one-on-one prayer. Encourage them to share what blessing in their lives is seeming more important than the blessor right now, or what they need to give to the Lord (knowing that God only asks us to give something up in order to bless us with something better later). Give kids three minutes to share and then ask them to pray for each other for the duration of Chris Tomlin's "Enough."

CLOSING (OPTION 2: PERSONAL COMMITMENT)

Pass out some index cards and ask students to write down on one side what they feel they should be surrendering to God and on the other side two steps they can take to make that happen. Ask the students to keep the index cards in a private place but somewhere they can be routinely reminded of their commitment. As they fill these cards out, play Chris Tomlin's "Enough."

CLOSING (OPTION 3: GOD'S ISAAC)

Have Chris Tomlin's "Enough" ready to play in the background. Before the meeting prepare a PowerPoint slide show with the information listed on **God's Isaac** (page 96).

Say something like,

> *Ultimately, it seems that Abraham's test boiled down to this: Would Abraham love the blessing or would Abraham love the blessor? Likewise, for us the question remains, will we be more attached to the blessings or to the one who blesses us? Perhaps this last activity will help. Let's reflect on God's sacrifice for us.*

While the music plays, run the PowerPoint slideshow.

End the meeting by saying something like,

Though Abraham's faith was tested, God stopped him from actually sacrificing his son. Instead, centuries later God offered his own Son Jesus as the lamb to be sacrificed. What that means for us is—

• God doesn't love us on the basis of what we can sacrifice but on the basis of Jesus' full sacrifice.

• When God convicts us to give something up, he does it to bless us with something better.

• Through Christ we are assured that we will have the ultimate blessing—eternity with God himself. So we are free to sacrifice anything during this lifetime because in the light of eternity, we have nothing to lose.

LIFT BY FAITH, NOT BY SIGHT

WORST-CASE SCENARIOS

Come up with six creative worst-case scenarios that could occur in a pole-vaulting event. To get your sadistic juices flowing, one example is given.

1. During the sprint, the pole-vaulter trips.

2. _____

3. _____

4. _____

5. _____

6. _____

7. _____

TRUE STORY

National Junior Olympics: The crossbar was set at 17 feet. Michael Stone confronted the most challenging day of his pole-vaulting career in front of an audience of about 20,000.

From the age of 14 Michael began a very careful and regimented weight-lifting program. He worked out every other day with weights, doing some kind of running work on alternate days. The program was carefully monitored by Michael's coach, trainer, and father. Michael's dedication, determination, and discipline were a coach's dream.

That day at the national Junior Olympics, Michael Stone cleared 17 feet. As soon as he landed on the inflated landing mat and with the crowd on their feet, Michael immediately began preparing for his next attempt at flight. He had just surpassed his personal best by a few inches and was one of the final two competitors. As the day progressed, Michael successfully cleared the bar at 17 feet, 2 inches and 17 feet, 4 inches, yet at each attempt he showed no emotion.

As he lay on his back and heard the crowd moan, he knew the other vaulter had missed his final jump. Since the other vaulter had fewer misses, Michael needed to clear his last vault to win. A miss would get him second place. The bar was set at nine inches higher than his personal best. "That's only one inch off the national record," he thought. He began to get nervous. It was either the eruption of the people in the stands or the thump of his landing that brought Michael back to earth. On his back with that wonderful hot sun on his face, he could only envision the smile on his mother's face. He knew his dad was probably smiling too, even laughing. What he didn't know was that his dad was hugging his wife and crying like a baby in his wife's arms. He was crying harder than ever before, the greatest tears of all: tears of pride. People immediately swarmed Michael, hugging and congratulating him. He later cleared 17 feet, 6 ½ inches for a national and international Junior Olympics record. With all the media attention, endorsement possibilities, and swarming hordes offering heartfelt congratulations, Michael's life would never be the same. It wasn't just because he won the national Junior Olympics and set a new world record. It was simply because _____ !

• Do you think Michael Stone had blind faith? Why or why not?

• What did Michael Stone have that he could trust in?

LESSONS IN SACRIFICE

What do you think are the top three things the average Christian teen struggles to surrender to God? For example, partying and social life, dating and purity, etc.

Third most difficult to give up: _____

Second most difficult to give up: _____

Absolute most difficult to give up: _____

You have 15 minutes to research and answer one set of questions below.

GENESIS 22:1-5
1. More than 20 times since Genesis 12, God has talked to Abraham. What do you think this tells you about trusting God?

2. How would Isaac have to be sacrificed, according to the text?

GENESIS 22:6-14
1. Do you think Isaac knows that he's to be the sacrifice? Why or why not?

2. Do you think Isaac may have resisted his father?

3. What animal does Abraham expect in verse 8? What animal does God provide in verse 13?

4. This test confuses Abraham because God had promised great blessing through Isaac (Genesis 15:4-5). Usually, those things we find difficult to give up to God hold some kind of promise to us as well. Do you have such a thing in your life? Share.

GENESIS 22:15-19
1. In what ways does Isaac seem surprisingly like Jesus?

2. Do you ever feel as if God allows something to happen to you that seems unfair?

3. What is God's response to Abraham's faithfulness?

HEBREWS 11:17-19.
1. Why is God's order to sacrifice Isaac contradictory to his promise to Abraham?

2. Have you ever felt as if God convicted you to give someone up? Explain.

3. In verse 19 we read that Abraham reasons before acting. What does Abraham reason about that enables him to trust God with his own son?

A SERIES OF UNFORTUNATE EVENTS

God has blessed us in different ways. Make a list of what you feel are the five most important physical things God has blessed you with. Write one in each box provided.

QUESTIONS FOR DISCUSSION

- Which sacrifice was the easiest to make? Why?

- Which sacrifice was the hardest to make? Why?

MERE CHRISTIANITY

Read the following excerpt.

"Every faculty you have, your power of thinking or of moving your limbs from moment to moment, is given you by God. If you devoted every moment of your whole life exclusively to his service, you could not give him anything that was not in a sense his own already. So that when we talk of a man doing anything for God or giving anything to God, I will tell you what it is really like. It is like a small child going to his father and saying, 'Daddy, give me sixpence to buy you a birthday present.' Of course, the father does, and he's pleased with the child's present. It is all very nice and proper, but only an idiot would think that the father is sixpence to the good on the transaction. When a man has made these two discoveries, God can really get to work. It is after this that real life begins. The man is awake now."—C. S. Lewis, on faith

According to the passage why is there technically no such thing as a sacrifice for God from Abraham?

GOD'S ISAAC

Prepare a PowerPoint slideshow to play at the end of the meeting. On each slide present the following paired statements and if you prefer, type out the actual Bible verses as well. To complement the effect include music such as Chris Tomlin's "Enough" and allow the text to appear and disappear using the dissolve mode.

Isaac is the promised seed (Genesis 17:16).
Jesus Christ is the promised seed (Galatians 3:29).

Isaac's birth was a miracle (Genesis 17:17-19).
Jesus' birth was a miracle (Matthew 1:18-25).

Isaac, the son of Abraham, was to be sacrificed (Genesis 22:1, 2).
Jesus, the Son of God, was to be sacrificed (John 3:16).

Isaac carries the wood for his sacrifice (Genesis 22:6).
Jesus carries the wooden cross for his sacrifice (John 19:17).

Isaac was obedient to his father unto nearly death (Genesis 22:5-12).
Jesus was obedient unto death (Philippians 2:5-8).

A ram takes Isaac's place (Genesis 22:13).
Jesus takes our place (2 Corinthians 5:21).

LENTILS: FAR TOO EASILY PLEASED
SESSION 9

BIG IDEA

In a world where everything is on-demand, drive-through, and microwavable, God still speaks through the quiet and unchanging. Although God has given us a destiny and promise, we often compromise the divine for the mundane, like a bowl of red stewed lentils. This study will focus on impatience, anger, and treasuring God and will give students an understanding of the importance of patience in our journey of faith.

WHAT IS MY BIRTHRIGHT AS A CHRISTIAN?

"The Kingdom of God, the pearl of priceless value—that was what Jacob wanted and that was what Jacob had risked everything to get. He believed in that kingdom; he believed in God. It was by faith that Jacob saw this kingdom, not by sight, for at that time on earth there was nothing. There was only one person—Jacob, the grasper, the deceiver—who had cheated his brother out of his birthright and his blessing. Was he the man on whom the kingdom of God depended? No! The Lord himself would build his kingdom. It would not be built by the goodness of any man,

YOU'LL NEED
• Bibles
• pens/pencils
• ingredients for **Red Stew** (page 99)
• copies of **Timed Shortcuts** (page 103)
• copies of **Brother From the Same Mother Who Deceives You Like No Other** (pages 104-105)
• copies of **Reverse Bible Study** (page 106)
• copies of **"Angrrrrrrr!"** (page 107)
• copies of **Candlelight Scribe Devotionals: A Guide** (page 108)
• small Christmas wreath
• heavy-duty scissors

INTERESTING TIDBIT

The Nelson Impact Bible Study notes that in ancient Hebrew culture, the job of keeping a common pot for food was the responsibility of the firstborn son. As the oldest son, Esau had the duty of maintaining a common cooking pot for the rest of the family members and potential guests who needed food. The imagery of the younger brother Jacob cooking the stew instead of Esau, who preferred hunting, is therefore rich with symbolism. It indicates that Jacob had already taken on the role of the firstborn son, even before Esau sold him his birthright.*

* _In the Beginning: Genesis_, Nelson Impact Bible Study Series (Nashville, TN: Thomas Nelson Publishers, 2005), 63.

nor could it be stopped by the wickedness of any man. Jacob would rule, not because of anything he had done, but because God had ordained it. How would he rule? In this life and on this earth a crown would never be placed on Jacob's head, but one day a son would come from Jacob, on whose head a crown of thorns would be placed. This son of Jacob would secure the kingdom of God forever by the sacrifice of himself for sin. This son of Jacob would be exalted to the throne of God, where he would reign forever and ever, as the King of Kings and Lord of Lords. This son of Jacob would be the ruler and conqueror of all the earth. In him all the prophecies and blessings and promises to Jacob would be perfectly fulfilled. Who was this son of Jacob? It was Jesus Christ, the Son of God, who loved us and freed us from our sins by his blood, and made us to be a kingdom. To him be glory, honor, majesty, and dominion forever and ever. Amen."[13]

OPENER (OPTION 1: BIDDING FOR RED STEW)

Prior to the meeting prepare one bowl of red stew as outlined in the **Red Stew** sidebar on the next page. Bring out the pot and perhaps some bread. Allow your students to taste the stew and then say something like,

> _I know you are very hungry tonight, but there is obviously not enough for the whole crew. Here is what we are going to do. Without using money let's bid for the stew. You can bid for it creatively, such as with a little dance, an afternoon washing my car, or helping me look for sermon illustrations this Sunday. To kick things off we'll start bidding with a pen. Anyone have a pen?_

Continue the bidding, evaluating whether each subsequent bid is more valuable than the previous one. Do this for 10 minutes. Whoever has the highest bid (which must be honored) at the end of the 10 minutes wins the stew.

Say something like,

> _Sometimes when we're hungry, we get cranky and perhaps a little illogical. Just as you bid for this stew with possessions, there was a person in Genesis who did the same thing. The difference is that this person sold his birthright in exchange for this lentil soup. His name was Esau._

Read Genesis 25:19-34 together. Ask—

- _From the sound of the word, what do you suppose a birthright may have been?_

- _Have you ever done something similar? In what ways have you sacrificed long-term gain for immediate gratification? Do you have any regrets about doing that?_

- _What is the most money you would've paid for today's stew?_

13 Nancy E. Ganz, _Genesis: A Commentary for Children_ (Wapwallopen, PA: Shepherd Press, 2002), 299-300.

OPENER (OPTION 2: TIMED SHORTCUTS)

Let your students know that this activity is a timed event. They are to go to the next question on the handout whenever you shout out "Next!" Ask your students to stretch out their fingers and loosen up as this is going to be fast. Hand out copies of **Timed Shortcuts** (page 103).

As students are going through the sheet, give them about two minutes for each question. When your students finish, share answers in the large group. At the end of this opener ask your students,

Did you wish you had more time? How do you suppose it affects our relationship with God when the world is always shouting "Next!" at us?

Read together from Genesis 25:19-34. Ask something like,

What was Esau's "Next!"?

TRANSITION: WHAT IS A BIRTHRIGHT?

Say something like,

Before we get into the lentils and tomatoes of the lesson, let's discover what a birthright was.

Then share the following information with your students.

Cultures of the ancient Near East gave special honor and privileges to the oldest male born in the family. In Deuteronomy 21:17 the right of the firstborn was both material and symbolic. The first son was the "first sign of his father's strength" and was to be given a double share of all the father had. This birthright also included the privilege of becoming the head of the household and leader of the family after the father's death. Therefore, the birthright was extremely important; the oldest son received natural riches, along with the title and honor of the whole family and the legacy of the past. (For example, if a family had 40 sheep, the oldest son would receive 20 sheep, the second 10 sheep, and the third 10 sheep. Daughters received nothing.)

As a group gather in prayer and ask God to bless the lesson and meeting and quiet everyone's hearts.

RED STEW

Serves four

1 chopped onion

1 tbs. olive oil

1 tsp. butter

1/2 tsp. ground coriander

3 cloves garlic, crushed

1 cup red lentils

5 sliced cherry tomatoes

3 cups beef stock

1/2 lb. spinach

1 tsp. pepper

1 tsp. salt or to taste

In a large stewing pot sauté chopped onion in olive oil and butter with coriander until the onions are soft and browned. Add the sliced cherry tomatoes and sauté for three minutes. Add the crushed garlic along with the lentils, beef stock, salt, and pepper. Stir well and bring to a boil on medium heat. Reduce heat and simmer for 30 minutes or until lentils are tender. Add spinach 10 minutes before serving and salt as needed.

DISCUSSION (OPTION 1: BROTHER FROM THE SAME MOTHER WHO DECEIVES YOU LIKE NO OTHER)

Divide your students into groups of three to four and hand out copies of **Brother from the Same Mother Who Deceives You Like No Other** (pages 104-105). Assign a different section to each group and give them about 25 minutes to find the answers.

When they are done, ask a volunteer from each group to give a brief summary of their answers, then ask,

> *What do you think is the main point of today's lesson, and what is one major application we can all work on together?*

DISCUSSION (OPTION 2: REVERSE BIBLE STUDY)

Divide your students into two teams and hand out copies of **Reverse Bible Study** (page 106). Ask kids to study Genesis 25:19-34. Each team is to come up with nine questions, ranking them easy, medium, and hard, three for each category. Along with the questions, they must also provide the answers. When the students finish, have the two teams challenge each other with the questions.

When the students are finished going back and forth with their questions, ask them to share their summaries of the lesson from the end of the handout.

DISCUSSION (OPTION 3: "ANGRRRRRRR!")

Say something like,

> *Today we are going to look at anger, but before we start, let me say something. Let's not get fooled into thinking that our anger has to master us. Anger is a voluntary choice. For example, imagine you are yelling at your friend and going berserk, and suddenly his mom walks in asking what is going on. You would be much more inclined to stop than if she hadn't come in. Let's go a little deeper now and find out what God says about anger.*

Hand out copies of **"Angrrrrrrr!"** (page 107). Ask students to watch the following clip and think about what it reveals about anger. Play the initial clip from *The Return of the King* (episode three of the *Lord of the Rings* trilogy), where the ring is found in the bottom of the lake while two guys are fishing (start at the very beginning of the movie). End the clip when Smeagol finally turns into Gollum (marker 06:20, about six minutes). Have students answer the first two questions on the handout.

Lead youth through the Genesis and James questions. Then say something like—

• *Anger transforms people. In your opinion was Esau's anger selfish or out of a sense of justice?*

• *Look back at your last argument, fight, or quarrel. Why were you angry? In other words, what was it that you wanted but were not getting?*

• *Are you a violent anger or a quiet anger person?*

End with the roleplay. Notice that the four principles listed require a certain level of self-analysis and evaluation. Spend some time explaining the four principles and let the students know that these four principles are to be used in the role play simultaneously, not in any sequence.

TRANSITION

Say something like,

> As we close today's session, let's apply what we've learned. Let's realize that urgency has the power to blind and that anger always happens because we don't get something we want.

CLOSING (OPTION 1: CANDLELIGHT SCRIBE DEVOTIONALS)

This option entails students having personal devotions on their own time. There is no group activity for this option. To slow down students in their quiet times, ask for kids to do three devotionals in the next week as follows.

Say something like,

> Our brains are so conditioned to live at broadband speeds that even our hearts speed past God. This way of doing devotionals this week will force you to slow your heart to handwriting speed.

Hand out copies of **Candlelight Scribe Devotionals: A Guide** (page 108) and go over the instructions on the handout with kids so they know what to do this week for the devotionals.

CLOSING (OPTION 2: THE WREATH)

Before your meeting try to find a small Christmas wreath and heavy-duty scissors.

Instruct kids to sit in a circle. Say something like,

The words wrath, wraith, *and* wreath *come from the same original word. Wrath is anger; wraiths are ghosts who have anger and unresolved emotions; and this is a wreath. A wreath is all twisted up, and perhaps that's how some of us feel because of unresolved anger or issues. Let's bring these before our Lord in prayer.*

Tell the kids to pass the wreath around, and if they have anything that is causing them anger or wrath, share it. After a person shares, have him cut up some of the wreath with the scissors and place the cut twigs in the middle of the circle. Tell students to arrange the twigs in the shape of a cross as they go. After all the students have had a turn, ask them to pray together, saying something like, "Father, today I submit my anger to you as I untangle it from my heart." Close the prayer.

TIMED SHORTCUTS

Each of these questions is going to be timed. When your teacher says "Next!" proceed to the next question. Don't linger. Ready, get set, next!

Come up with as many "shortcuts" as you can that are designed to make life faster. (Here's a freebie: Fast-food drive-thru.)

Generally speaking, what are some positive and negative consequences of these shortcuts? Be as specific as possible.

How can shortcuts positively or negatively affect your relationships with other people?

How can shortcuts positively or negatively affect your relationship with God?

When should you use shortcuts and when should you not use shortcuts?

BROTHER FROM THE SAME MOTHER WHO DECEIVES YOU LIKE NO OTHER

Work on the section assigned to your group. You have about 25 minutes to find the answers. When you're done, come up with a summary statement for your section and pick a volunteer to give a brief summary of your answers to the other groups.

GENESIS 25:19-34

1. Who does Isaac marry when he turns 40?

2. What problem does Isaac's wife face that gets Isaac to pray to the Lord?

3. What's the first thing you do when you face a problem? How often do you pray to the Lord about your problems?

4. In verse 23 what does the Lord say to Rebekah about her babies?

5. Why is Esau named "Esau"?

6. Why is Jacob named "Jacob"?

7. How are Esau and Jacob different from each other?

8. What does Esau want from Jacob? What does Jacob want in return?

9. Why do you think a birthright is so important to Jacob, whereas to Esau it means nothing?

10. Did you ever take something for granted and not end up realizing what you lost until it was too late?

GENESIS 26-28

1. In 26:7 after the Lord has told Isaac to stay in Gerar, the men there ask questions about his wife. What does Isaac say to them?

2. We saw a similar incident and response occur before Isaac's time. Who was this other person? (Hint: Look in Genesis 12:10-13 and Genesis 20:1-2.)

3. Both Isaac and the person above weren't able to trust in the Lord with their lives, even when God said he would be with them. Do you sometimes have doubts about what God has promised you?

4. Who does Esau marry and where is she from? Are Isaac and Rebekah pleased? Why or why not?

5. In 27:2-10 what is Rebekah's plan for Jacob when Isaac is about to give his blessing?

6. What are the two things that Esau loses to Jacob?

7. Overall, what are Jacob's and Esau's blessings?

8. When is the last time you got violently angry? What happened?

9. Where and to whom does Jacob have to go because of his brother's anger over the blessing?

10. What does Isaac specifically tell Jacob to do and not to do before he leaves home?

REVERSE BIBLE STUDY

In your team study Genesis 25:19-34 together and come up with nine questions, ranking them easy, medium, and hard. Place three questions in each section. Along with your questions, also provide answers. When you are finished, prepare to challenge the other team and see who grasped the text best.

Easy
1.

2.

3.

Answers:

Medium
1.

2.

3.

Answers:

Hard
1.

2.

3.

Answers:

Summarize the lesson into a short paragraph that answers these three questions:
• What is the main point of the text?
• How do we experience this text today?
• What is a practical application of this in my life?

Lesson summary:

"ANGRRRRRRR!"

As you watch the video clip and read from the following texts, answer the following questions.

ANSWER BY YOURSELF

From *The Return of the King*
1. Why did Smeagol kill his fishing buddy?
2. How did Smeagol change over time?

Read Genesis 25:29-34, 27:5-10, and 27:30-41.
1. Why was Esau angry?
2. What did Esau finally desire to do to Jacob?

Read James 4:1-3.
1. According to James, why do people fight and argue?
2. According to James, what was the cause of Esau's anger?

FOUR SIMULTANEOUS PRINCIPLES

1. Analyze something that angers you by asking yourself, "What am I not getting that I really want?" (James 4:1)
2. Ask God to satisfy your real need. (James 4:2)
3. Is this anger selfish or out of a desire for justice?
4. Extend the time between anger and your response (yelling, cursing, etc.).

ROLE PLAY

If you're up to it, volunteer to share your most recent moment of anger. If necessary, ask someone to act as the other party and reenact the event.

Now reenact the event again, but use the four simultaneous principles as you go along.

CANDLELIGHT SCRIBE DEVOTIONALS: A GUIDE

INSTRUCTIONS

• Find a candle, light it, and turn off the lights.

• Open up in prayer, but as you're praying, write down your prayer (preferably in your journal).

• Read one of these Bible texts: Luke 10:38-42, James 4:1-10, or Genesis 25:19-34. Use a different one for each of three devotional times this week.

• Write down the whole text of the Bible verses on paper.

• Write down the answer to "God, I feel you are telling me to..." (and be specific as possible).

• Write down the answer to "God, this is what I want to do this week..." (and be as specific as possible).

BIG IDEA

This lesson is a study of Jacob as a deceiver. God has to wrestle him down to change his heart. Only then does Jacob's name change from deceiver to overcomer—but at a cost: an eternal limp.

ZIPPED FILE

Begin the lesson by saying something like,

I think we can agree that we all struggle with God. Truth be told, we are committed to make it big in life. Furthermore, I think we can also all agree that sometimes we are afraid of the unknown. As a result we sometimes lie and deceive others. Let's begin today by reviewing the life of someone who experienced these exact things. His name was Jacob.

Hand out copies of **Jacob's Life: Zipped File** (page 113) and review it with your students. Then proceed to the Opener options.

YOU'LL NEED

- Bibles
- pens/pencils
- copies of **Jacob's Life: Zipped File** (page 113)
- videorecorder and blank tape
- copy of **Masters of Deception** (page 114)
- TV
- copies of **Slo-Mo-Spontaneo Script** (pages 115-116)
- copies of **WWJD (World Wrestling Jacob Disclocation** (page 117)
- copies of **Deceiver to Overcomer** (pages 118-119)
- index cards
- copies of **Master of Truth** (page 120)

OPENER (OPTION 1: MASTERS OF DECEPTION)

This activity is a video scavenger hunt/special effects challenge. Before the meeting prepare a video recorder and blank tape and charge the recorder. Tell kids that they'll have to use their ingenuity and figure out ways to do special video effects with a camcorder. If you have more than one camcorder and enough students, make additional groups.

Ask one person to be the designated camera person and give out one copy of **Masters of Deception** (page 114) to each team (if you split into smaller groups).

When the students are finished, plug into a TV or projector or watch directly from the LCD display on your video recorder. Make sure you keep track of points. Award a special gift to the team with the most points (if you had more than one team).

When the group finishes this activity, say something like,

> *This activity was called "Masters of Deception" because it focuses on your using smarts to create illusions and tricks. In the Bible there is one character who can also be called a master of deception. His name is Jacob. The difference here is that although our deceptions were humorous, his deceptions almost got him killed a number of times. Let's dive in and meet this master.*

OPENER (OPTION 2: SLO-MO-SPONTANEO)

Ask for four volunteers from the group and let them know that you will be doing a slow-motion spontaneous reenactment of Genesis 32:22-32. Give each student a copy of **Slo-Mo-Spontaneo** (pages 115-116) and explain that one person will be the narrator, the second person will create the special sound effects, and the final two will play God and Jacob. The narrator reads the bulleted script.

Let the volunteers know that they are to reenact what the narrator reads, but in slow motion. Encourage kids to lower their voices as in slow-motion footage.

TRANSITION

Say something like,

> *I think it's pretty safe for us to say that God isn't finished with us yet. There are things in our lives that God doesn't want us to leave unresolved, and because of those things, sometimes he has to corner us and wrestle us down to the ground. But one thing that we can be sure of is this: Whenever God decides to wrestle us down, we will never be the same. Let's look at how we can apply Genesis 32 to our lives.*

DISCUSSION (OPTION 1: WWJD (WORLD WRESTLING JACOB DISLOCATION))

Start by asking questions like—

- *Have you ever been cheated by someone? Describe what that experience felt like.*

- *How do you suppose God wrestles with us in modern times?*

- *How do we win or lose when we wrestle with God?*

Divide your students into groups of three or four and hand out copies of **WWJD (World Wrestling Jacob Dislocation)** (page 117). Assign a different section to each group and give them about 25 minutes to find the answers.

When they're done, ask a volunteer from each group to give a brief summary of their answers and share their summary statement for the section. Write their summary statements down on a large poster or marker board.

As a whole group attempt to come up with the answer to the following question: "Why did God wrestle with Jacob?"

DISCUSSION (OPTION 2: DECEIVER TO OVERCOMER)

Hand out copies of **Deceiver to Overcomer** (page 118-119) and allow kids about 10 minutes to match the verses to the characters. Here are the correct answers, in chronological order:

(1. Satan deceives (Genesis 3). 2. Abraham deceives Pharaoh in Egypt (12:13). 3. Abraham deceives in Gerar (20:2). 4. Isaac deceives in Gerar (26:7). 5. Jacob's name means "deceiver" (27:36). 6. Jacob deceives his father (27:21-29). 7. Laban deceives Jacob into marrying Leah (29:23). 8. The 10 brothers deceive Jacob about Joseph's fate (37:32). 9. Joseph deceives his brothers about his identity (42:9).)

Allow kids to continue with the Make It Personal section. Once they complete it, have them share their answers. Then have students continue with the Make It Live! section and have them share their answers to "What can you do now in response?"

TRANSITION

Say something like,

The only way we can be masters of truth is if we know that Jesus took care of all our punishment and secured for us the greatest blessing: eternity in heaven with him. In fact, God has sent the Holy Spirit into our lives and still wrestles with us today when he senses we're going back to deceptions and lies. Perhaps you feel him wrestling in your heart about something right now. This last activity will help you face your challenge.

CLOSING (OPTION 1: WRESTLING WITH GOD)

Hand out index cards to your students and on one side have them write out the words of Luke 22:42. On the other side have students write down how they feel God is wrestling with them. Ask the students to memorize the passage before they leave and challenge them to apply what they wrote down. Ask them to keep the cards in their Bibles until they have faced their challenges.

End in prayer.

CLOSING (OPTION 2: MASTER OF TRUTH)

Hand out copies of **Master of Truth** (page 120) to your students. Ask them to think of and write down a deception or lie that is pressing on their hearts. Allow kids to fill out the cards and challenge them to make amends by the date on the cards. Ask them to keep the cards in their Bibles until they have faced their challenges.

End in prayer.

JACOB'S LIFE: ZIPPED FILE

In Genesis 25:23 God introduces and foretells the course of Jacob's and Esau's lives. From birth Jacob is a deceiver and overtakes his older brother, Esau. In Genesis 25:29-34 we read about how he takes advantage of Esau's hunger to cheat him out of his birthright for a bowl of red lentil stew and later on how he tricks Isaac into giving him the family blessing (Genesis 27:1-40). As a result Esau hates Jacob and plans to kill him, forcing Jacob to flee for his life and hide out with his uncle Laban (27:41-45).

On his way, however, God speaks to Jacob in a dream and promises to bless him with descendants, honor before the world, and safety (28:13-15).

When Jacob reaches Laban, he falls in love with Laban's daughter Rachel. Laban therefore takes advantage of this situation by taking seven years of indentured servitude from Jacob in exchange for his daughter. When the seven years are over, Laban tricks Jacob by substituting his older daughter Leah for Rachel. When Jacob understands what has happened, he's furious but resigned to serve seven additional years out of his love for Rachel. Jacob and Laban then spend six additional years trying to outsmart each other for more livestock (30:25-43). Eventually, Jacob decides to flee from Laban, but his father-in-law overtakes him. For Jacob's sake God intervenes and prevents Laban from harming him.

In an effort to reconcile with Esau, Jacob sends some of his servants to bribe Esau with wealth, but they return with the news that Esau is coming with 400 men. Jacob prays to God for protection (32:9-12). The night before he has to face Esau, Jacob meets God in a wrestling match and fights all night long (32:24). Even though God dislocates Jacob's thigh with a touch (32:25), Jacob continues to hang on to God and refuses to let go unless he is blessed. God therefore blesses Jacob and changes his name to Israel (32:28). Now ready to meet Esau, Jacob passes everyone to meet Esau directly (33:3), and in a miraculous turn of events, the twins reconcile. Jacob eventually returns to Bethel where God renews his covenant promise once again (35:11-15).

MASTERS OF DECEPTION

Get ready to film. For this exercise you will have to use your smarts and ingenuity to figure out video special effects worthy of Hollywood! Pick someone to be the designated cameraman and get rolling.

MANDATORY ITEMS, NO POINTS
Each of you needs to introduce yourself on the video by saying your name, age, school, and favorite thing to smell.

As a group run toward the camera in slow motion and blow kisses at the camera.

As a group read John 3:16 in unison.

POINTS: 10,000 PER ITEM
With the people in your group, figure out a way to capture a stadium "wave" of 50 fans.

Have your group stand on one person's hand.

Viper spit: Have someone strike a kung-fu pose and squirt "venom" out of her mouth. The victim gets the "venom" splashed onto her face and dies.

Have a student fly through a shower of white meteors that look surprisingly like crumpled paper.

POINTS: 15,000 PER ITEM
Have one person wiggle into another person's mouth and get swallowed up.

Have one person call a spaceship and disappear.

Have someone use "the force" and "raise" a Bible from the ground up into his outstretched hand.

Have one person throw a plastic knife. Another person should catch the knife with the blade inches from his face with his palms.

SLO-MO-SPONTANEO SCRIPT

HERE ARE THE RULES:

1. One person narrates the bulleted items.

2. One person does the special sound effects.

3. One person plays the stranger (God).

4. One person plays Jacob.

The Bible verse numbers are included, but the narrator should only read the bulleted lines. Pause between bullets to allow the actors to respond. Some strange events are included; just do your best to act everything out.

ORIGINAL VERSE: 22

• It's a dark, ominous night...wind is howling. In the distance a dog barks...like a cat.

• Jacob waves bye-bye to his two wives, two maidservants, and 11 sons.

• He then crosses the Jabbok River.

ORIGINAL VERSE: 23

• He also sends all his earthly possessions over the river.

• That strange dog barks again...like a snake.

ORIGINAL VERSE: 24

• So Jacob is left all alone.

• Out of nowhere a man jumps him. They wrestle for hours.

• And hours. That strange dog barks again.

• Jacob and the stranger are caught in a wrestling match to see who'll give in first.

• Jacob seems to be winning.

• Then the stranger starts coming back. Regardless, Jacob will not let him go.

ORIGINAL VERSE: 25

• But the stranger cannot overpower Jacob, so he touches him near his thigh.

• Jacob's hip is wrenched out of the socket, causing incredible pain and agony.

ORIGINAL VERSE: 26

• Then the stranger says, "Duuuuuude, let me gooooo."

• But Jacob replies, "Not unless you blesssss me."

• Besides the voices of the two men, the only other sound is the gurgling of the river.

ORIGINAL VERSE: 27

• The stranger asks Jacob for his name.

• Still in pain, almost in tears like a little baby, Jacob squeals his name.

ORIGINAL VERSE: 28

• Now the rooster is beginning to make his usual morning noise.

• The man says, "Your new name's Israel, 'cuz you struggled with God and men and overcame."

ORIGINAL VERSE: 29

• Jacob says, "What's your name, dude?"

• In the background the wind is roaring.

• "None of your business" replies the stranger.

ORIGINAL VERSE: 30

• Jacob gets up and says, "I saw God face to face and—whoa!—I'm still alive!"

• He looks around and decides to call the place Peniel.

ORIGINAL VERSE: 31

• As the sun is rising with the usual sound that the sun makes while it rises...

• Jacob walks away limping.

• In the distance a dog barks.

WWJD (WORLD WRESTLING JACOB DISLOCATION)

Work on the section assigned to you. You have about 25 minutes to find the answers. When done, pick a volunteer to give a brief summary of your answers to the other groups. Also come up with a summary statement for your whole section.

GENESIS 29-31

1. What does Jacob ask for when Laban offers him a wage?

2. From what 29:17 says, what do you think Leah looked like compared to Rachel?

3. How many total years does Jacob have to work for Rachel?

4. Which of his two wives does Jacob love more?

5. In what way does Jacob cheat Laban in 30:37-43?

Summary statement: _____

_____

_____

GENESIS 32

1. Why do you think Jacob sends his two wives, maidservants, 11 sons, and possessions away from himself?

2. What does the man do to paralyze Jacob?

3. How has Jacob struggled with men and overcome?

4. What does "Peniel" mean?

5. In what ways can you identify with Jacob?

Summary statement: _____

_____

_____

DECEIVER TO OVERCOMER

MATCH THE VERSE TO THE PEOPLE

Read the verses on the right and match each one to the people or person involved in that verse.

Joseph deceives his brothers about his identity.   Genesis 12:13

The 10 brothers deceive Jacob about Joseph's death.   Genesis 27:21-29

Jacob deceives his father.   Genesis 3

Abraham deceives in Gerar.   Genesis 20:2

Satan deceives.   Genesis 26:7

Isaac deceives in Gerar.   Genesis 29:23

Jacob's name means "deceiver."   Genesis 42:9

Laban deceives Jacob into marrying Leah.   Genesis 37:32

Abraham deceives Pharaoh.   Genesis 27:36

MAKE IT PERSONAL

As you can see, the book of Genesis is filled with masters of deception. It seems that whenever there are tense situations to face, the main characters of Genesis always resort to some kind of trickery. After Jacob wrestles with God in Genesis 32, however, Jacob seemingly begins to change. After the wrestling match, Jacob faces his greatest fear.

Below list some fearful situations or people you have to face. Explain why the situation is worrisome.

I am worried about facing _____

because _____

I am worried about facing _____

because _____

I am worried about facing _____

because _____

MAKE IT LIVE!

When Jacob wrestles with God, it seems as if he's transformed from a deceiver to an overcomer. In fact, the next day Jacob faces his brother Esau, whom he tricked twice out of a birthright and a blessing. Why this transformation? Jacob realizes that he has fought God and survived. Imagine that. In Jacob's eyes nothing is scarier than God; therefore, he could now face all things. In fact, *Israel* means "God fights." In other words, God now fights for Jacob.[14] Jacob now depends on God to be his fighter.

People lie and deceive because they want illegitimate gains or are afraid of punishment. The Bible says that God already has heaven stored up for you and that he has taken the ultimate punishment for your sins. On the cross God fought for you and won!

What can you do now in response?

14 Boice, James Montgomery, *Genesis: An Expositional Commentary*, vol. 1 (Grand Rapids, MI: Baker Books, 1982).

MASTER OF TRUTH

My latest lie/deception was when I:

As I believe that God is wrestling in my heart about this, I will face this by

_____   _____
month/day   signature

PUT ME IN YOUR BIBLE!

MASTER OF TRUTH

My latest lie/deception was when I:

As I believe that God is wrestling in my heart about this, I will face this by

_____   _____
month/day   signature

PUT ME IN YOUR BIBLE! ·

MASTER OF TRUTH

My latest lie/deception was when I:

As I believe that God is wrestling in my heart about this, I will face this by

_____   _____
month/day   signature

PUT ME IN YOUR BIBLE!

JOSEPH AND SEX
SESSION 11

BIG IDEA

Everyone is talking about it. Everyone is thinking about it. What is it? S-E-X. This session is designed to address temptation and sexual purity in an X-rated world by discovering the nature of lust and its behavior.

During the lesson students will:

- learn what lust is and about its behavior.
- study God's view of sex.
- learn the importance of community in our struggle against lust.
- understand sexual struggle in the context of our relationship with God.
- learn where to find comfort when we fall in our sexual struggles.

YOU'LL NEED

- Bibles
- pens/pencils
- room you can make completely dark
- jellybeans
- copies of **Unexpected Ends** (page 126)
- the movie *Fantasia*
- copies of **Joseph in Egypt** (page 127)
- copies of **A Chronicle of Lust** (page 128)
- copies of **Best Defense Is a Good Offense** (page 129)
- cupcakes and candles
- matches
- copies of **Less Than...Human!** (page 130)

OPENER (OPTION 1: LIGHTS ON, LIGHTS OFF)

Some things are easier to do in the dark, and when the lights are back on, it's easy to conceal who did what. For this exercise find a room that will turn completely dark once the lights are turned off, such as a basement. (Make sure you have at least two adults present for safety and liability reasons.) Gather the students in a circle and lay out a mound of jellybeans in the middle of the circle, within easy reach of the students. Pick three students to take turns as light bearers (kids new to the group would be best). Have the first light bearer stand near the light switch, facing the wall, and instruct him to turn the light off, count five seconds, and turn the light back on. While the lights are off, tell the kids in the circle to reach over and take as many jellybeans as they want, either none or some. After the lights come back on, the light bearer should rejoin the group and guess how many students actually took jellybeans and of those who took some, how many jellybeans they took. The light bearer who guesses the most correct wins the rest of the jellybeans.

Ask questions like—

- *What can you do to make the light bearer guess wrong?*
- *What are some other things people usually do secretly, in the dark?*
- *Once the lights are back on, is there a way to determine with certainty who grabbed jellybeans?*

Say something like,

> There are countless things we struggle with, and we have a hard time confessing a vast majority of them to people. What's more, we would probably never carry through with many of our sins if people were present right next to us. This is one of the benefits of living in community with each other. We must push to develop in our church or small group this kind of community, where with the presence and encouragement of others we can grow and effectively fight back against some temptations. We need to become lights in each others' lives.

OPENER (OPTION 2: *FANTASIA* MOVIE CLIP)

One section of Walt Disney's *Fantasia* is a rendering of a 1779 poem by Johann Wolfgang von Goethe called "The Sorcerer's Apprentice." Hand out copies of **Unexpected Ends** (page 126) and read the stanza together, starting with, "Off they run, till wet and wetter...."

Ask the students to watch the movie clip from *Fantasia* and write down as many similarities as they can between lustful (or addictive) behavior and scenes in the movie clip.

Start the clip where the wizard is conjuring up a spirit (scene 6, marker 29:47). Mickey is seen coming downstairs carrying two buckets of water. End the clip when the wizard snatches the hat back from Mickey and scolds him with the broom (marker 39:04, about 10 minutes).

At the end of the clip have kids share their thoughts on lust. They might have noted that—

(Mickey used his eyes and fantasized about power. Mickey waited to be alone. When Mickey attempted to destroy the broom, it multiplied. The condition quickly got out of hand. A stronger outside person (the sorcerer) had to come in to stop the mayhem.)

Note: This opener is not meant to endorse magic or the occult. Make sure the students understand this. Furthermore, the sorcerer at the end seems to be angry at Mickey. Remind your students that unlike the sorcerer, our heavenly Father is a God of love. You may want to point out that the sorcerer had to scold Mickey out of love, not disdain.

Answer the questions at the end of the handout as a group.

TRANSITION

Say something like,

Today we are going to talk about lust and how it works. I know this may be a somewhat private topic, but I encourage you to be as honest and open as possible. At the same time let's be confidential. Whatever we say in here stays in here. Let's begin by getting acquainted with Joseph.

Hand out copies of **Joseph in Egypt** (page 127) and review the material together.

DISCUSSION (OPTION 1: A CHRONICLE OF LUST)

Say something like,

There are a few places in the Bible where we as readers can make some educated guesses about people's personalities based on their behavior and actions in special situations. In this account we learn much about both Joseph and Potiphar's wife. Let's see if we can make some educated guesses about them.

Ask some questions like these:

INTERESTING TIDBITS

Throughout Joseph's life the Lord doesn't speak directly to him. Until about Genesis 36, the Lord is directly involved in the lives of the main characters through speech (God speaks to Adam, Eve, Noah, Abraham, etc.) and intervention (God creates, God brings a flood, stops Abraham from sacrificing Isaac, wrestles with Jacob). Some points to note—

• Joseph was very attractive (Genesis 39:6).

• Nameless wife: Though most of the people in the account of Joseph's life have names, this woman is nameless. She is simply "his master's wife" (39:7).

• Potiphar: captain of the bodyguard. A high official in the government of Egypt, specifically of Pharaoh's personal guard. He was among the trusted men of Pharaoh and perhaps something of a prime minister. His name in Hebrew may mean he was a eunuch.

• Who would the sin be against? Joseph sees any sexual misconduct with Potiphar's wife as an offense to Potiphar, but primarily to God (39:9).

continued next page

Interesting Tidbit cont.

• Relentless temptation: Joseph has to face this temptation from Potiphar's wife repeatedly. Notice that regardless of the number of attempted seductions, Joseph does not compromise (39:10).

• Location, location, location: One of Joseph's strategies is not to get caught in the wrong place at the wrong time. For him that means he refuses being geographically close to Potiphar's wife, and when he's cornered, he runs. (1 Corinthians 6:18: "Flee from sexual immorality.")

• When accused, Joseph doesn't defend himself or plead his case. He remains silent (39:13-19).

• Joseph doesn't get killed. In both Near Eastern and Egyptian law, adultery was punishable by law, and the penalty was death. And the sin was much worse when a slave was accused of sleeping with his master's wife (39:20).

• Though it seems as if Joseph goes from bad to worse, notice that the Lord is watchful and blessing Joseph with kindness and favor among those he's with (39:21-23).

• *Have you ever experienced the hurt or anger of being turned down or dumped? Based on your experience, what kind of people do you think Potiphar's wife or Joseph may've been?*

• *Do you think Potiphar's wife was in love with Joseph? Why or why not?*

• *Do you suppose Potiphar's wife may have been promiscuous?*

Hand out copies of **A Chronicle of Lust** (page 128). Break the kids into small groups and give them 15 minutes to answer the questions. There are more questions than time allows. Feel free to pick seven (or more, or less) out of the entire set that you feel address the needs of your group. Gather back together and discuss the answers to the questions on the handout.

DISCUSSION (OPTION 2: BEST DEFENSE IS A GOOD OFFENSE)

Hand out copies of **Best Defense Is a Good Offense** (page 129) and give kids 10 minutes to complete it. When they finish, have students discuss the results of the questionnaire section to the degree that they feel comfortable.

Review the answers to Strategic Living together. Allow students to formulate their own "best defense is a good offense" strategy for purity and share openly.

TRANSITION: CHRIST-CENTERED

Say something like,

Just like Potiphar's wife, we live in a society that seems to come at us relentlessly with images and attempts at seduction. If the statistics are right, there's a very strong chance that some of us regularly struggle with lust and sexual impurity. Perhaps a few of us don't even struggle anymore; we have already thrown in the towel of surrender and live in fear or shame. But we can be encouraged today.

The Scriptures say that Christians can be confident and not discouraged. Though purity may not be easy, God accepts us on the basis of our trust in the crucified and living Savior, not based on our performance. In Christ there is "now no condemnation" (Romans 8:1).

Joseph was imprisoned for sins he didn't commit. Potiphar's wife lusted and Joseph paid the penalty. The reason Joseph wasn't executed (according to law) was that someone from his own family would take the ultimate punishment for the lust of our hearts. Jesus was executed on the cross. Regardless of where you are or what you have done, know that in Christ you are pure and blameless.

CLOSING (OPTION 1: CUPCAKE TIME)

End with cupcake time. Say something like,

As we end today, let's have some time of reflection and sharing. Let's get together with members of the same gender and share and pray over this lesson together.

Before the lesson prepare one cupcake per every two kids and place a candle in each cupcake. Have kids pair off and give each pair a candled cupcake. Find some mellow Christian music to play in the background and have teachers/volunteers go around and light the cupcakes. As much as possible have students pair off with those they know least well. Tell students that as long as their candles are lit, they are to talk and share about themselves. Have one partner share for half the candle and the other share for the other half. Tell students to share struggles, things they're joyful about, and about their family and friends. Once the candle is finished, allow students time to pray for each other and share the cupcake.

CLOSING (OPTION 2: LESS THAN...HUMAN!)

Hand out copies of **Less Than...Human!** (page 130). Read and discuss the C. S. Lewis quotation and give students enough time to discuss the questions that follow. Give your students enough time to flip through the various passages and answer the questions concerning location and accountability. Discuss the importance of these two, and if you are able, share some personal experiences. Ask kids to reflect on the lesson and come up with their own strategies for purity by completing the final sentence, "To stay pure I can..." If some students are willing, ask them to share their answers.

UNEXPECTED ENDS

Some of you may not know this, but part of Disney's *Fantasia* came from an old poem by Johann Goethe written in 1779. We'll read the following excerpt from "The Sorcerer's Apprentice" together.

Off they run, till wet and wetter
Hall and steps immersed are lying.
What a flood that naught can fetter!
Lord and master, hear me crying!
Ah, he comes excited.
Sir, my need is sore.
Spirits that I've cited
My commands ignore.
Johann Wolfgang von Goethe, 1779 (translation by Edwin Zeydel, 1955)

As you watch the clip, try to list as many similarities between the story in *Fantasia* and lust (or addiction) that you can think of.

FANTASIA	LUST

WE'LL ANSWER THE FOLLOWING QUESTIONS AS A GROUP.

• Why do you think Mickey waited to be alone?

• What do you think the moral of the story is?

• Did you ever start something in secret that quickly got out of your control? Without going into details (unless you want to share), how did you feel about it? Did you ask for help?

JOSEPH IN EGYPT

In Genesis 37 we meet Joseph as a teen. We discover that he's a favored son of Jacob and as such, he received a special coat from his father. In his dreams Joseph has a prophetic vision of his own brothers and family bowing down before him. Perhaps unwisely, he tells his family about these dreams, which leads to a dramatic turn of events; his jealous and now angry siblings decide to sell Joseph to a group of Ishmaelites on their way to Egypt. Potiphar, a captain of the guard, one of Pharaoh's high officials, then purchases Joseph as a slave from the Ishmaelites. In Potiphar's house God blesses Joseph in all he does, and because of his sharp managerial abilities and support from God, Joseph finds favor in his master's eyes. All seems to be going well (relatively speaking) for Joseph, but now God allows for a twist of events...Joseph faces the lusting of a woman.

A CHRONICLE OF LUST

Find the answers to the following questions and learn practical things you can do to safeguard yourself and grow in purity. Before you begin, read Genesis 39 aloud together. Have the guys read the odd verses and the girls the even verses.

GENESIS 39: 1-10

1. How much power does Joseph have in Potiphar's household?

2. In verse 6 we discover that Joseph is attractive. How much does physical appearance influence your choice of pursuing someone?

3. What reasons does Joseph give for choosing not to sleep with Potiphar's wife?

4. Do you think Joseph has an accountability partner? Who?

5. How often does Potiphar's wife try to seduce Joseph? What do you suppose this tells you about Potiphar's wife and Joseph's impact on her?

VERSES 11-19

1. In what ways does Joseph not compromise when it comes to sexual temptation? List three.

2. We have no account of Joseph defending himself in the text. Why do you think this is so?

3. Potiphar doesn't inflict upon Joseph the just punishment for adultery, which was death. What do you suppose this may reveal about Potiphar and/or Joseph?

VERSES 20-23

1. In what ways do you think God is working through this whole chapter in Joseph's life? Make a list.

2. How does the ending of Genesis 39 echo the beginning of it?

3. Do you see any resemblances between Joseph and Jesus? List as many as you can.

BEST DEFENSE IS A GOOD OFFENSE

Know that this is your own personal copy. During the discussion you can share as much or as little as you want about the answers below. Make sure that you are honest with yourself. Fill out the following form by marking an X under the column that is closest to the way you feel.

	NEVER	KINDA	50%	OFTEN	ALWAYS
I am careful about the images I allow into my head.					
I struggle with purity.					
I imagine provocative or romantic situations.					
I check out guys/girls at the mall.					
I hang out with friends who desire purity.					
I avoid places where I could be tempted.					
I am careful to wear clothing that doesn't turn heads.					
I memorize Scripture that deals with lust/sex.					
I read Christian books on the topic of dating/purity.					
I go to a small group where I am comfortable talking about anything.					
I flirt with members of the opposite gender.					
I am careful with how I touch members of the opposite gender.					
I have quiet times.					
I meet regularly with an accountability brother/sister.					
I talk to my accountability brother/sister about sexual stuff.					
I pray on a regular basis.					
I am careful with what magazines I read.					
I am careful with what I watch on television/ movies and listen to.					

STRATEGIC LIVING

From eyes to fantasize: In verses 6 and 7 we read that "Joseph was well-built and handsome...and after a while his master's wife took notice of Joseph." The original language implies that Joseph is attractive and that Potiphar's wife is checking him out top to bottom with her eyes and her mind.

• Can you think of a time when there was a particularly powerful visual image that stayed with you? Explain.

• Do you think fashion today encourages "eyes to fantasize"? Share.

• Where do you see a lot of sexual imagery today?

LESS THAN...HUMAN!

In *The Four Loves*, C. S. Lewis says about lust that "We use a most unfortunate idiom when we say, of a lustful man prowling the streets, that he 'wants a woman.' Strictly speaking, a woman is just what he does not want. He wants a pleasure for which a woman happens to be the necessary piece of apparatus. How much he cares about the woman as such may be gauged by his attitude to her five minutes after fruition (one does not keep the carton after one has smoked the cigarettes)."

According to Lewis, lust turns a person into a mere "apparatus," a *tool* for pleasure.

• How does Genesis 39:17-18 reveal the woman's intentions toward Joseph?

• What do you think the difference between love and lust is?

LOCATION, LOCATION, LOCATION!
The account seems to hint repeatedly at the importance of location. What do the following verses reveal?
• Genesis 39:10

• Genesis 39:11

• Genesis 39:12

• 1 Corinthians 6:18

In what ways can you apply this truth?

ACCOUNTABILITY
When Joseph is tempted, he responds by describing his relationship to Potiphar himself (verses 8 and 9). Joseph feels trusted and accountable to someone.
• What do you think are the difficulties and benefits of having an accountability partner?

• What kind of person makes a good partner in faith?

PUTTING IT ALL TOGETHER
According to the above, write a strategy for how you can stay pure in today's lustful society.

To stay pure, I can _____

BIG IDEA

This lesson will teach students to remain confident in the Lord regardless of what their situations may look like. In the life of Joseph, God used what others intended for harm for his glory and the rescuing of many.

OPENER (OPTION 1: SHOWING FAVORITISM)

As students settle in, introduce the lesson by showing a one-minute clip from *Titanic*. Begin with scene 20 (rewind about one second to marker 1:56:16), when, as the *Titanic* is sinking, Molly says, "Come on, you heard the man. Get in the boat, sister." End the scene as Cal says, "Not the better half" (marker 1:56:50).

Say something like,

Showing favoritism hurts those who are not favored. In Titanic *the result is the deaths of thousands of people. Today we're going to continue looking at the life of Joseph. Let's read Genesis 37. One thing is certain: Favoritism leads to problems.*

YOU'LL NEED

- Bibles
- pens/pencils
- the movie *Titanic*
- ice cream treats
- copies of **X-Man** (pages 137-138)
- tape
- two posters or sizable paintings
- black-and-white scans of the posters or paintings
- copies of **Joseph's Life: Zipped File** (pages 139-140)
- copies of **Good Luck, Bad Luck** (page 141)
- 8.5" X 11" sheet of paper
- candles

continued next page

You'll Need cont.

• recordings of slow worshipful music

• index cards

• cross

• copies of **A Testimony of Pain** (page 142)

• cups of grape juice

• pieces of bread

INTERESTING TIDBITS

Silent but active

Throughout the book of Genesis God continually speaks and acts in sometimes spectacular ways. He speaks with Adam, Noah, Abraham, and others. God sends a flood (Genesis 6-8) and a firepot with blazing torch (Genesis 15:17) and wrestles with Jacob (Genesis 32). Interestingly, from the beginning of the Joseph narrative God seems to quiet down. The narrative of Joseph's life teaches us that although God's presence may sometimes seem undetectable, he is nonetheless acting powerfully.

Key role of Joseph in Israel's history

God chose Joseph in his plan to preserve and prosper Israel throughout the great

continued next page

Joseph was shown favoritism, and this favoritism almost got him killed.

After you read the chapter, ask something like—

• *Have you ever experienced being passed over for someone else? How did you feel about it?*

• *Have you ever experienced being the one favored over others? How did you feel about that?*

OPENER (OPTION 2: CRUEL YOUTH LEADER)

Tell your students that you received free jackets (of a cool brand or style, depending on what your knowledge of youth culture is). However, let them know that there are only three jackets available (or any number less than your total group size). Say something like,

A friend of mine who owns a clothing company gave me three free jackets, but we have to interrupt our small group now and immediately go get them. He has all the sizes but can only give me three jackets. So I'm sorry, but I decided to give the jackets to (names of kids). We'll be right back. Stay here.

Take out the students you named and come back a few minutes later. Perhaps you can come back with ice cream or some other treat for all the kids.

When you come back, let the group know that there were no such jackets...just ice-cream treats for all. Ask the following questions:

• *Have you ever experienced being passed over for someone else? How did you feel about it?*

• *Have you ever experienced being the favored one over others? How did you feel about that?*

TRANSITION

Say something like,

Although Joseph suffered for being 'special,' his brothers marked him for death. Out of the 50 chapters in Genesis the life of Joseph spans almost 14, by far the longest chronicle of any other in Genesis. But maybe not—perhaps the account of Joseph's life is supposed to point us to the real hero of the story, God. By getting an overview of the life of Joseph, let's see whether we can learn some things about God himself.

DISCUSSION (OPTION 1: THE X-MAN)

This exercise will give students a general overview of the life of Joseph.

Say something like,

> *I realize that perhaps some of us are not artistic, but today's lesson will require some drawing. Having said that, the flow of your story is more important than the drawing.*

Hand out copies of **X-Man** (pages 137-138). Have your students make their own versions of a comic book page from the given list of 11 verses. As there are only 11 boxes, allow students to pick and choose situations within the 11 options and determine which are the most significant for the flow of the text.

Give kids about 25 minutes and remind them to focus their attention on the flow of the story rather than the artistry of the drawings. If space allows, tape the completed drawings up on a wall. Ask students to volunteer and explain why they chose to represent Joseph's life as they did. In a discussion format, ask kids to share their answers to the questions included on the **X-Man** sheet.

DISCUSSION (OPTION 2: JOSEPH'S LIFE: ZIPPED FILE)

Find two posters or sizable paintings, the larger the better. (If you live near a Staples or a Kinko's, print out some black-and-white pictures to the largest size possible.) Keep the posters concealed before your meeting.

Before breaking out into smaller discussion groups, ask for two volunteers, one girl and one guy, and blindfold them. Say something like,

> *Let's determine who has a better understanding of life, guys or girls.*

Ask one of the two students to step outside the meeting room. Position the other blindfolded student directly in front, as close as possible to the poster/picture. Remove the blindfold and ask the youth to decipher what the picture represents. Have her describe what she sees.

Very slowly, have the student move away from the picture. Every inch or so ask whether she has a better idea of what the image is. Continue to do this until she recognizes the image. Repeat this exercise with the second student and determine who recognized the image first. Make sure you have a means to measure the student who recognized the picture first.

Say something like,

continued next page

famine in the land of Canaan. Though Joseph experienced great turmoil and injustice in his own life, God planned all that happened to him for the good and salvation of many. While in Egypt, Israel grew to become a wealthy and powerful nation, setting up the stage for their exodus 400 years later under the leadership of Moses.

Richly ornamented robe

The Hebrew translation for *ketonet passim*, "richly ornamented robe," is nebulous and disputed. What commentators agree on, however, is that the robe was long enough to reach his hands and feet. Though interpretations vary, it is agreed that long robes differentiated nobility from the working class as shorter robes were better suited for manual labor. Egyptian and Syrian artwork from that period does, however, support the possibility that the coat may indeed have been "richly ornamented."*

* The JPS Torah Commentary on Genesis (Philadelphia: The Jewish Publication Society, 1989), 255-256.

Sometimes when we're in the thick of our situations, it's hard to see what God is doing. Sometimes we need to wait and take a few steps back to see the bigger plan of God in our lives. It is important that we get a general overview of Joseph's life to understand the sovereignty of God and his plan for good. Genesis 50:19-21 states the main theme of the whole Joseph narrative. The following discussion cuts to the chase of the lesson.

Hand out **Joseph's Life: Zipped File** (pages 139-140) and read the condensed version of Joseph's life story together. After reading the story, ask kids to complete the Bad to Best section. Allow students about 10 minutes and then share answers.

Read Hebrews 12:7-11 and share a personal life illustration of the verses with your kids. Then have kids finish the handout and review their answers.

TRANSITION

Retell the story **Good Luck, Bad Luck** (page 141) and say something like,

Unlike the farmer in the story, we can have confidence. Today's lesson taught us that in the end, because of God's sovereignty and favor toward his people, we will experience much more than simple good luck. We will experience blessings and prosperity. Perhaps this may not happen in this lifetime for many of us. But Scripture gives us an awesome picture of what the future holds. As Joseph's suffering blessed the Israelites, the suffering of Jesus promises us the ultimate blessing.

CLOSING (OPTION 1: PATH OF JOSEPH)

Print out on separate sheets of 8.5" x 11" paper the words and Bible texts listed below in the given order, one per sheet. If time allows, make the first sheet of paper crumbled or partly burnt; toward number 12, make the sheets more beautiful or ornate.

Preferably in a separate room, place the sheets of paper along the ground to make a prayer path. Depending on how many students you have and how much space is available, provide a number of these paths. On each sheet place a candle. Turn down the lights as dim as possible and have slow, worshipful music playing. If you choose, allow two students to take the path at any time, walking along opposite sides of the paper path. As students reach each "station," have them turn to that text in their Bibles and meditate on it. At the end of each path place a cross and some index cards. Tell kids to write prayers on the index cards and place the cards under the cross.

1. TAKE REVENGE.   MATTHEW 5:38-42

2. CRY.   PSALM 28:1-2

3. BLAME GOD.   MATTHEW 27:45-46

4. CURSE. JOB 2:9

5. COMPLAIN. DEUTERONOMY 1:27

6. RUN AWAY. PSALM 139:7-10

7. DRINK/OVERINDULGE. PROVERBS 23:20

8. PUSH THROUGH/KEEP DOING THE RIGHT THING. JAMES 1:2-4

9. TRUST GOD. JOHN 14:1

10. PRAY. PHILIPPIANS 4:6

11. READ SCRIPTURE. 2 TIMOTHY 3:16-17

12. RECEIVE BLESSING THROUGH SUFFERING. ROMANS 8:28-30

CLOSING (OPTION 2: TESTIMONY OF PAIN)

Have students flip through the verses listed below. Ask them to pick the two verses that most resonate with their present situations and difficulties. Hand out index cards and ask the students to write out the text on one side and the verse on the other. Encourage them to memorize the Bible verse in the following week, and if you wish, offer a special prize for those who successfully memorize their verse(s). Hand out A **Testimony of Pain** (page 142). Have kids read the story and then ask some questions like—

• *How are physical pain and emotional suffering because of life circumstances similar?*

• *What do you think God's purpose for pain in our lives is?*

• *How can we make difficult moments in our lives more bearable?*

BIBLE MEMORY CARDS

Genesis 50:19-20	Hebrews 12:11	Philippians 4:4-7
Hebrews 12:5-6	Romans 8:28	James 1:2-3
Hebrews 12:7	Romans 8:31-32	

CLOSING (OPTION 3: LOVE FEAST DUOS)

Note: Before you go through with this option, make sure that it does not break any constitutional laws of your denomination.

On a separate table prepare small cups of grape juice and pieces of bread. Have slow prayer music playing in the background. Ask kids to pair up. Bring each pair two small cups of grape juice and two small pieces of bread.

Say something like,

Out of the tragedy of the cross came the blessing of eternal life and intimacy with God. Spend some moments sharing whatever hardships you may be going through. As each of you finishes sharing, the other person should break a piece of bread, dip it in the juice and say, "Christ took the ultimate suffering that you may be blessed. May God's blessing renew your heart." Then the other person goes. End your time lifting each other up to God in prayer.

USING THE FOLLOWING VERSES, SKETCH OUT A COMIC BOOK VERSION OF THE LIFE OF JOSEPH.

Genesis 37:3-11
Genesis 37:19-36
Genesis 39
Genesis 40
Genesis 41
Genesis 42
Genesis 43
Genesis 44
Genesis 45
Genesis 47
Genesis 50:15-21

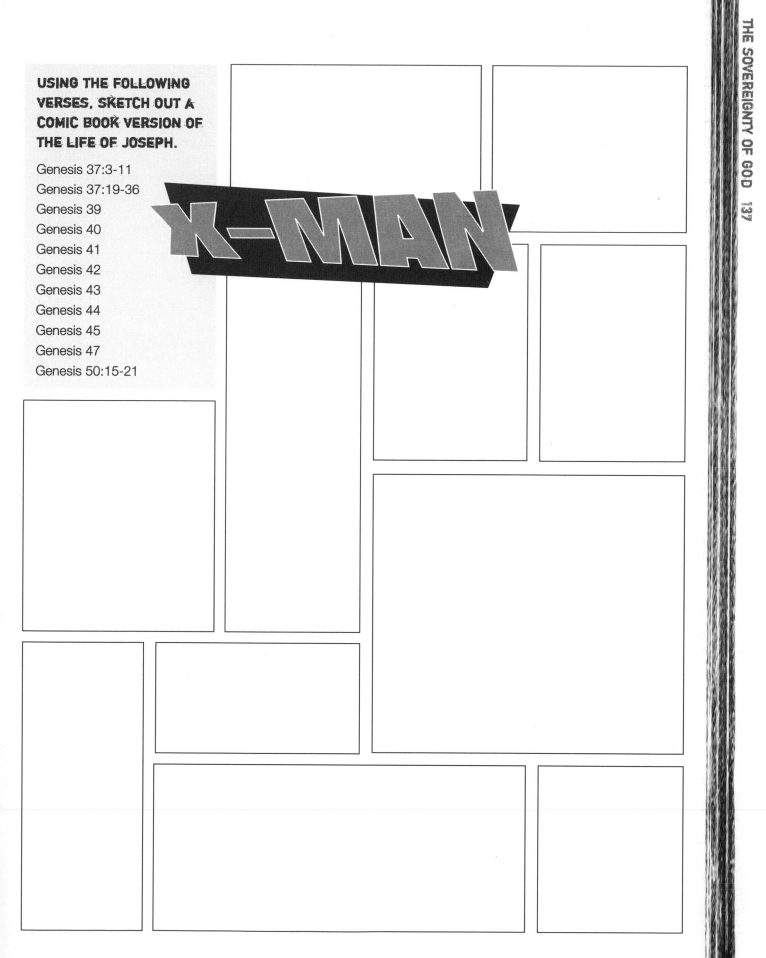

ANSWER THE FOLLOWING QUESTIONS:

1. Throughout the life of Joseph how visible was God?

2. In what major ways do you think God worked in the life of Joseph?

3. Who benefited the most from Joseph's hardships?

4. What practical thing can you do when you feel as if God is distant?

JOSEPH'S LIFE: ZIPPED FILE

Here is a condensed version of the life of Joseph: Joseph was Jacob's favorite child. He also had dreams in which wheat sheaves representing his brothers bowed down to him. His brothers, therefore, became jealous and developed a hatred for Joseph. His brothers sold him into slavery in Egypt where eventually his master's wife falsely accused him of rape. As a result Joseph was thrown into prison, but God blessed Joseph so that he rose to prominence even in prison. While in prison, Joseph interpreted the dreams of two of Pharaoh's servants. Later on, because of this very gift, he was called on to interpret Pharaoh's dreams. Joseph foretold that a famine would come in seven years. Pharaoh noticed that Joseph was blessed with wisdom and understanding and put him in charge of all of Egypt to prepare for such a famine. In due time the famine spread over the earth, but Joseph had built up huge grain supplies in Egypt. Back in Canaan, Jacob heard that there was food in Egypt, so he sent his sons to Egypt to buy grain. Although they bought grain from Joseph, they didn't recognize their own brother, and Joseph kept his identity secret during the brothers' next two visits to Egypt. In an emotionally tense scene Joseph revealed himself to his brothers and instructed them to return to Egypt with their families and their father, Jacob. Jacob came to Egypt where Joseph provided good land for the families to live on. When Jacob died, his family took his body back to Canaan for burial. Once Jacob was gone, Joseph's brothers feared that Joseph would take revenge on them. But as a summary of Joseph's life, he explained that what they intended for harm, God had planned for good.

BAD TO BEST

If there is a simple idea to capture the life of Joseph, it would be going from "bad to best." Perhaps the most important verse of the Joseph account is Genesis 50:20-21:

You intended to harm me, but God intended it for good to accomplish what is now being done, the saving of many lives. So then, don't be afraid. I will provide for you and your children." And he reassured them and spoke kindly to them.

IN THE TABLE BELOW WRITE EXAMPLES OF BAD TO BEST IN JOSEPH'S LIFE, JESUS' LIFE, AND YOUR LIFE.

BAD	TO BEST
Joseph was sold to Ishmaelites as a slave.	The Ishmaelites sold Joseph to a powerful man in Egypt, and Joseph did well.
Joseph was accused of rape.	
Jesus died on the cross.	
Your examples:	

READ HEBREWS 12:7-11.

• What is the "bad to best" in these verses?

• What do these verses encourage us to do?

• What does suffering reveal?

GOOD LUCK, BAD LUCK

The Chinese tell the story of a farmer who used an old horse to till his fields. One day the horse escaped into the hills, and when the farmer's neighbors sympathized with the old man over his bad luck, the farmer replied, "Bad luck? Good luck? Who knows?" A week later the horse returned with a herd of horses from the hills, and this time the neighbors congratulated the farmer on his good luck. His reply was, "Good luck? Bad luck? Who knows?"

Then when the farmer's son was attempting to tame one of the wild horses, he fell off its back and broke his leg. Everyone thought this was very bad luck. Not the farmer, whose only reaction was, "Bad luck? Good luck? Who knows?"

Some weeks later the army marched into the village and conscripted every able-bodied youth they found there. When they saw the farmer's son with his broken leg, they let him off. Now was that good luck or bad luck?

Who knows?

Author Unknown[15]

15 *Hot Illustrations*, www.youthspecialties.com.

A TESTIMONY OF PAIN

Nobody ever enjoys a painful moment, whether physical or mental. Through the weekly workouts and races during the track and cross-country season, I find it especially difficult trying to prepare myself for these physical and mental abuses during practice. Although the workout tests my physical and mental strength and endurance of pain, I know that in the end these instances of agony make me stronger and more prepared for races. I find these meetings with pain mentally and physically prepare me for the next big event. I also believe that God creates and gives us painful situations in life to strengthen us for the future. With this idea in mind, although I may not see the immediate purpose for a challenge that God sets before me, I trust and know that God is in control and is doing what is best for me.

Also, through experiencing pain, I find myself praying to God and depending on him for comfort and relief. Before every workout or race I mentally prepare myself by praying to God to give me strength through the situation and to help me make the most of every moment in that opportunity. By viewing pain with this outlook, I don't dread the imminent agony but see it as a short price to pay for a much greater reward.

Pain to me is also a very humbling experience. Pain exposes my weaknesses, and often at that moment there's nothing I can do to hide them. I believe that God subjects me to pain to show me how dependent I am on him. In learning my weaknesses, I see that no matter how independent or firm I think I am, God reveals another weakness to me. Although I don't enjoy painful moments, I understand the necessity behind them and try to work my way through them diligently. Even though it may be difficult, I try to see pain as a blessing and an opportunity to mature.

Phil, student from Philadelphia

BIBLIOGRAPHY

Bartholomew, Craig G. and Goheen, Michael W. *The Drama of Scripture: Finding our Place in the Biblical Story*. Grand Rapids, MI: Baker Academic, 2004.

Boice, James Montgomery. *Genesis: An Expositional Commentary*, vol. 1. Grand Rapids, MI: Baker Books, 1982.

Boice, James Montgomery. *Genesis: An Expositional Commentary*, vol. 2. Grand Rapids, MI: Baker Books, 1982.

Boice, James Montgomery. *Genesis: An Expositional Commentary*, vol. 3. Grand Rapids, MI: Baker Books, 1982.

Currid, John D. *A Study Commentary on Genesis*, vol. 1. Webster, NY: Evangelical Press, 2003.

Currid, John D. *A Study Commentary on Genesis*, vol. 2. Webster, NY: Evangelical Press, 2003.

Davidson, Robert. *Genesis 1-11*. Cambridge: University Press, 1973.

Davidson, Robert. *Genesis 12-50*. Cambridge: University Press, 1979.

Goldsworthy, Graeme. *According to Plan: The Unfolding Revelation of God in the Bible*. Downers Grove, IL: Intervarsity Press, 1991.

Hays, J. Daniel. *From Every People and Nation*. Downers Grove, IL: InterVarsity Press, 2003.

Hoekema, Anthony A. *Created in God's Image*. Grand Rapids: MI: Wm. B. Eerdmans Publishing, 1986.

Lewis, C. S. *Mere Christianity*. New York, NY: HarperCollins, 2001.

Piper, John. *Desiring God*. Sisters, OR: Multnomah Publishers, 1986.

Ridderbos, Herman. *The Coming of the Kingdom*. Philadelphia, PA: P & R Publishing, 1962.

Robertson, O. Palmer. *Christ of the Covenants*. Phillipsburg, N.J: P & R Publishing, 1981.

Roop, Eugene F. *Believers Church Bible Commentary: Genesis*. Scottdale, PA: Herald Press, 1987.

Ryken, Leland; Wilhoit, James C.; and Longman III, Tremper. *Dictionary of Biblical Imagery*. Downers Grove, IL: InterVarsity Press, 1998.

Vangemeren, Willem. *The Progress of Redemption*. Grand Rapids, MI: Baker Books, 1988.

Williams, Michael D. *Far as the Curse is Found: The Covenant Story of Redemption*. Phillipsburg, NJ: P & R Publishing, 2005.

Wolters, Albert M. *Creation Regained: Biblical Basics for a Reformational Worldview*. Grand Rapids, MI: Wm. B. Eerdmans Publishing, 1985.

In the Beginning: Genesis. Nelson Impact Bible Study Series. Nashville, TN: Thomas Nelson Publishers, 2005.